An Italian Boy's Life

An Episodic Memoir

Frank J. Tassielli

Dedication

This memoir is dedicated to my three sisters, Maria Carmela, Grazia and Antonia who died at age 13, 4 and 2, respectively. They represent a sad past.

It is also dedicated to my three grandchildren, Alexa, Nick, and Danielle, who were born in 2002, 2006 and 2007, respectively, and who represent a bright future.

Finally, I am dedicating this memoir to my mother and father, Angela Rosa Spano Tassielli (1909-1992), and Massimiliano Tassielli (1908-1990), who loved me unconditionally.

Contents

Acknowledgements

Writing and self-publishing a book about my life and my family's history has long been a dream of mine. I have always felt that it is important to connect with the people of the past who sacrificed so much for us to have a better way of life. Along the way, there have been many people who have encouraged and inspired me. To all my friends and family members who've listened to my many stories over the years, and who have given me support for this project, you know who you are and I will be forever grateful to you.

Having the thoughts and the desire to write a memoir is one thing; however, actually getting started and proceeding with the writing, proof-reading, re-writing, and still more re-writing is quite another. When I first enrolled at Stony Brook University's Round Table (as it was then called) immediately following my retirement in 2001, several people mentioned the Memoir Writing class. It wasn't until several years later that I finally enrolled in the class, and by then the organization was called OLLI (Osher Lifelong Learning Institute). From the first moment I set foot in the class, its leaders, Dorothy Schiff Shannon and Sheila Bieber, impressed me by the manner in which they led the class. Their organizational skills, strong support and encouragement, along with the constructive criticism of many other members of the class, allowed me to continue my writing. Their comments and input into my writing are much appreciated, so thank you, Sheila and Dorothy.

Since much of the family history I have written about occurred either before I was born or while I was an infant, I have had to rely on anecdotes from many of my cousins and, in some cases, my cousins' children.

To all my cousins who fielded my many, many questions over the years, I would like to say thank you for sharing all your stories. And I also have to make a special mention of my "big sister" Mary who, because she preceded me on this earth by a full six plus years, has been able to recall people and events that have proven invaluable in the telling of my story. So, thank you, Mary, for sharing.

As I neared the end of my writing, I realized that perhaps the next obstacle could be the most formidable: Using my feeble computer skills to check all my fonts, set up a format, include all my photos through a scanning process with which I am unfamiliar, transmitting my entire manuscript electronically and a number of other computer-related tasks. As frustration began to mount, along came a God-send: I had lunch in the spring of 2012 with a former student of mine, and from the beginning she whole-heartedly accepted the computer-related responsibilities of my project. To Christine Fiore Hecht, an eternal thank you for your expertise but more so for your alacrity in taking on this task. You have my undying gratitude.

A heartfelt thank you to all of you; I hope you enjoy reading my memoirs.

Introduction

In writing this book of personal memoirs I have attempted to communicate the emotions I felt and still feel deep inside me. These emotions, particularly regarding the memories of my early life in Italy, and of which I have few recollections, were borne mostly out of the conversations I have had with numerous family members over the years. Their distant memories of my family were instrumental in compiling the following memoirs. Included are stories about my family and myself that were often difficult to write in that the depths of my feelings, my inner soul, if you will, was what I hoped to reveal. You, the reader, will decide if I have succeeded.

The format that I have chosen to write my book is episodic. Although the sections have not been separated into two distinct areas, the fact is that this book does deal with two distinct features: my family members and their history, individually and otherwise, and episodes and relationships from my own life. Some episodes will follow a previous one chronologically and cohesively, while some may be intermingled with others and do not necessarily relate to each other except for the fact that I experienced them.

I would further like to state unequivocally that I have always felt both blessed and fortunate in two significant aspects of my life.

The first is the fact that I arrived in the United States at such an early age that the transition from one language to another, one culture to another, was experienced with a minimum of pain. Knowing the difficulty in assimilating that both of my parents, who were in their thirties, and my older sister, who was twelve, and so many of my cousins, aunts and uncles as well as millions of other immigrants who had to assimilate themselves into the American way of life, language and culture, I often remind myself of my good fortune. Second, I was also blessed to have had the opportunity to avail myself of the excellent educational system America offers.

Rarely does a day pass that I don't think that the life I've led was denied to three of my older sisters, and the older I get, the more I try to savor and cherish the life I have been given. This gift was denied to my sisters Maria Carmela, Grazia and Antonia, who died at such an early age. During the telling of these stories, I've occasionally repeated or overlapped recollections. This book that I've dedicated to them should in no way diminish that story.

A main goal of my book has been to inform all the generations that followed my father's and mother's parents. I believe that we need to know our roots for spiritual, historical and even medical reasons. Such stories, not written, could otherwise pass into dust. Hopefully, my children, grandchildren, and the progeny that follow me will understand the full depth of emotion that I have carried within me for all of my life.

It is my fervent hope that my children, Frank and Sharon, and my grandchildren, Alexa, Nick, and Danielle, understand that the life they have been given as citizens of this wonderful country of ours would not have been possible if not for the sacrifices of my mother and father, Angela and Massimiliano Tassielli.

I hope you enjoy "An Italian Boy's Life."

An Italian Boy's Life

An Episodic Memoir

Years of Hardship

She was alone. Not since he had gone off to war in North Africa eight years earlier had Angela felt this sense of loneliness. However, back in 1932, that separation was for only seven months and Maria Carmela was their only child. But now it was 1940 and Meline (Maria Carmela's nickname) had three younger sisters: Maria, the next oldest, was six years old; Grazia Laura was four and Antonia was two. Angela was also five months pregnant, and hopeful that her fifth child would be a boy, which would please her husband, Massimiliano.

Her husband's departure, although sudden, was expected. Many men in the village had done the same thing. That fact, however, did not diminish Angela's feelings of loneliness. Who would her support system be? She had no money; Massimiliano had left none because there was none. Her mother had died when Angela was just nine years old and although her father had re-married and her step-mother was a good woman, the mother-daughter bond was simply not there.

Angela herself was the youngest of three girls. Her older sister Catherine had three young children of her own and her husband had already been gone to America for ten years. Her middle sister, Donata, who was married to a man considerably older than she was, had six children of her own. Of course, there was her husband's mother and father, and when she became desperate during that miserable fall of 1940, she begged them for whatever morsels they could spare, only to find that they too suffered the same deprivations. In addition, their daughter and her two young children were living with them and bore the further burden of having a husband who was a prisoner of war of the British. Indeed, they weren't even certain that he was still alive.

So as the summer of 1940 came to an end, Angela's fifth child, a boy, finally was born to her and Massimiliano. Thanks to the mid-wife who lived just a few doors away the birth was without complications. The boy was named Francesco, naturally, which was her father-in-law's name. There was no choice in these matters. Tradition was always upheld.

It was almost six months now since he had left, and there had been no letters from him. She wanted desperately to communicate to her husband that he was now the proud father of a son. Communication of any sort, however, was not so easily accomplished between Europe and America in 1940 due to an event called World War II.

In 1932, when Massimiliano was serving in Il Duce's army in North Africa he had contracted malaria and was sent home with a medical discharge. His time away from home had been less than a year. Now, though, he was in America, looking to make a better life for himself as his older brother Nick had done twenty years earlier. Those years between 1932 and 1940 were difficult ones. They scratched out a meager living, as so many families did in Southern Italy. The work was long and hard for the men, laboring as many as twelve to fourteen hours under the hot sun, cultivating the soil, planting, harvesting and pruning, all for enough money to barely feed his growing family. The land was not theirs; it belonged to wealthy land-owners who lived like kings while the overwhelming majority of the workers, Massimiliano among them, toiled for next to nothing, and grateful for the opportunity. It would be many years later when he would tell his adult son that he felt like a slave to these landlords.

Timing, it is often said, is everything. Massimiliano was the youngest of three boys. The oldest, Vincenzo, who was born in 1895, was in America working to build America's transcontinental railroad alongside his father when he was summoned to return to Italy in 1916 to serve in the Italian Army. Several months later he was wounded in battle and succumbed to the injury within a few days; he was twenty-one years old. Four years later, the middle brother, Nick, left for America by himself. He was nineteen years old and would eventually marry, raise four children and become a successful businessman in New Jersey. However, the politics and prejudice resulting from America's huge immigrant influx of the early twentieth century led to the passing of the National Origins Act in 1924, which severely limited the numbers of Southern Italians, Greeks and other Southeastern Europeans that could legally enter the United States.

So as 1939 passed into 1940, with Mussolini and Hitler rampaging through Europe, Massimiliano feared he would once again be drafted into the Italian Army. He knew he had to do what many other men in the village had done before him. He had to take a chance. He had to find a way to get to America. Along with three fellow stowaways he made a difficult ocean crossing, living like a dog, he would say years later, in a tiny closet in the hold of the steamship. All during this voyage, however, he had pangs of regret. How could he leave his wife and four young daughters for an indeterminate period of time? When would he see them again? Assuming he made it safely to America, how would he be able to send money to his family, money that he had been told hung from trees waiting to be plucked by hard-working individuals?

All Angela knew was that somehow she had to feed her five children, and the winter of 1940 was closing in.

It was now mid-November and all five of her children were either fighting colds or other assorted ailments. What exactly were they suffering from? Medical intervention was pretty much limited to local midwives and other mothers who had seen their own children through these sicknesses. But the two younger girls, Grazia and Antonia, were getting worse; they were feverish. The time-tested treatments of well-meaning friends and neighbors were not helping.

Antonia, who was two, was a bubbly child who had begun speaking just a few weeks earlier. Her fever was the worst. Crying late into the night, she begged her mother to carry her outside to see and feel the snow that had begun falling. Snow in Southern Italy was a rare occurrence, and Angela, though hesitant to expose Antonia to the chilly night air, relented. Antonia's face lit up when she tasted the snow flakes and felt them fall on her burning face and forehead. Angela felt she had done the right thing.

Before the sun rose the next morning, however, Antonia was dead. Angela was beyond shocked. The girl had had a fever, yes, but how was she to know that it had deteriorated into pneumonia and sapped whatever strength the child had left, snuffing the life out of her on November 27, 1940. She was two years old.

The subsequent burial took place after a full day of viewing. As was the custom, Antonia's body lay on the kitchen table in the room that served as a kitchen, bedroom, and dining room. Incidentally, there was no running water, and the apartment had no bathroom. After twenty-four hours, the child's body was laid to rest in the village cemetery.

Grief-stricken, Angela had little time for grieving. Her newborn son, Francesco, was also burning up, as was Maria, now six, and Grazia, four. Meline, the oldest, was fine. Fine, that is, if one could call an eight year old child who was obviously retarded, incontinent, unable to walk and talk and basically stopped developing at the age of ten months. And so she was fine, not suffering from chills and fevers like the other children.

Barely three weeks had passed when tragedy struck again. This time it was Grazia who had succumbed to what some in the village called Typhus. On the morning of December 21st, Grazia was laid to rest alongside her baby sister Antonia. Angela went through the motions; she was numb. Which of her children would be the next to die? Where was her husband? Why hadn't she received any correspondence from him? It had been almost nine months since he had left her. Did he make it to America? Did he find work? Why hadn't he sent her money? Had he abandoned her and their children? That wasn't possible, was it? She was reeling with self-doubt.

The emptiness and despair that Angela felt in the months that followed were beyond my ability to describe in words. It was only many years later that I began to understand the depths of those feelings, and my understanding was not nearly enough.

Angela's Pain

My mother lived through a haze for all of 1941. Two of her daughters had died. Her pain and agony was felt by every fiber of her being, and yet she had to stay strong while her infant son Francesco and seven year old Maria struggled through colds, fevers and malnutrition. Somehow, Meline, who was now eight years old, maintained her physical strength. Though unable to speak, barely able to walk and incontinent, she somehow avoided the ailments her younger siblings contracted. Because she had a tendency to wander off and get lost due to her incapacitation, she had to be restrained by either being tethered to a bed post or tied to a chair, for hours at a time. The support of Angela's sisters, sister-in-law, neighbors and friends was incalculable.

Massimiliano had not been heard from since the day he left, more than a year earlier. As 1941 became 1942, Angela was still without any communication from her husband. Mussolini's Fascism had become entangled with Hitler's Naziism and Italy's postal service was one of its casualties. She had to assume he had made it safely to America. With war clouds churning throughout Europe and America's entry into this global conflict in full force, she knew that most channels of communication between America and Europe were practically non-existent. And so she lived day to day. Her faith in God remained strong and her daily prayers to the Almighty were a part of her ritual. She knew that God would see her through the tragedies that had befallen her and her family.

It was late spring of 1942 when the postman delivered a letter from America. Angela was overwhelmed with emotion as she read the return address. It bore her brother-in-law's name and New Jersey address. Tearing open the envelope and seeing the familiar handwriting of her husband, tears streamed down Angela's cheeks as she read the words aloud, very slowly.

———◆———

"My Dear Angela,

Please forgive me for not writing for such a long time. I wrote you several letters shortly after my arrival here in America, but when I received no reply I knew the war was the reason. My voyage to America went without incident, and I am safe here with my brother Nick and his wife Anna. I am in good health and working in a local factory. I hope to save enough money so that when this terrible war ends I can send for you and our beloved children. Please give all of them kisses from their father, who misses them very much.

How is our newest child? Is it a boy or a girl? And how are the girls doing, especially Meline? Are my mother and father helping you out?

My brother Nick and his wife Anna have been wonderful the whole time I have been here. Within a few weeks after my arrival I was able to get my own apartment in Newark, just a couple of miles from Nick's house. I eat dinner with them almost every night. America so far has proven to be an exciting country with lots of jobs available.

And now for the best news possible: I was advised by several paisans, as well as by Nick, that I should take advantage of the United States government's offer to grant amnesty and US citizenship to illegal aliens like myself if I would voluntarily serve in the US Army, and so I enlisted this past weekend. I am excited to tell you this because the sergeant at the recruitment office told me that Italy's and Mussolini's alliance with Hitler is not going well and the days when our country is occupied by the Nazis is going to be short-lived. Hopefully, by the time you receive this letter, I will be a US citizen in a US Army uniform. The best part of all this is that within a few months, the sergeant assured me that I would be able to have part of my monthly pay sent to you. All of this depends on what happens the next few months, but I am hopeful.

I am not sure how long it will take for you to receive this letter, but write back to me in care of Nick's name and address as soon as you can. You cannot know how much I miss and love you and our children.

Your loving husband,
Massimiliano"

———————

Angela held the letter close to her breast, with tears streaming down her cheeks. The next-door neighbor had come to the door when she heard the screams, and now, she too was screaming with joy as Angela told her of the news from her husband in America.

Within a couple of hours, her parents, sisters and the rest of her family and in fact the entire neighborhood knew of the letter. Two more letters came from her husband that summer. Massimiliano was by then a Private First Class in the United States Army! In that time Angela had written her husband of their daughters' deaths.

By the end of 1943 Mussolini had fallen and the Germans were being pushed northward by the advancing Americans and the Allies, who had landed in Sicily, crossed the Straits of Messina, and were now on the Italian peninsula.

Events started to move very quickly for Angela. One of Massimiliano's letters contained a name, address and document that would allow her to shop at an American Post Exchange that had been recently set up in Bari, just six miles away. That information, along with the allotment check that had arrived just days earlier, meant that almost everything had changed dramatically for Angela and her family.

By the spring of 1944, Massimiliano's letters were coming regularly and had included specific instructions as to how Angela and her children could arrange for transportation that would take them to America. The Allies had successfully landed in France on June 6th, and victory over Germany was within reach. Once Hitler's armed forces surrendered, Massimiliano explained to her, America and her allies would assemble all their energies toward the defeat of the Japanese. Hopefully, within a year or so, the world would be at peace once again and safe passage to America would follow.

Angela was elated, but her concern was now focused on her oldest daughter, who was severely disabled and would probably not gain entry into the United States. Angela's concern turned to tortuous quandary.

"If my husband wants us to join him, and Meline is forced to remain in Italy, what am I to do?"

These dark thoughts led to her writing a letter to Padre Pio, who was known throughout Italy as "the priest of miracles"; Padre Pio had borne the wounds of the crucified Jesus for many years, and was venerated throughout Italy.

A local teacher helped Angela formulate a letter to Padre Pio. In it she asked for wisdom for her plight. Within a couple of weeks Angela received a response. In his letter the saintly priest blessed this woman who had experienced such tragedy and told her that God, in His infinite wisdom, would find a solution for her. That solution came in the summer of 1944 when Meline died in her sleep. The wake and burial that followed left Angela with mixed emotions. She prayed to her Madonna that, as the Blessed Mother, she would embrace her dearly departed child, as she had her other young children, Antonia and Grazia, who had died four years earlier.

The fall and winter of 1944 were filled with excitement as letters from America and her beloved husband arrived almost weekly, as did the monthly allotment checks, which allowed Angela to buy goods that had been previously unavailable. America and the Allies' victory over

Germany were a foregone conclusion as 1945 arrived, although there was terrible news of unexpected victories by the Nazis in France. Still, victory was just weeks away, the world was told.

Massimiliano's letters were filled with anticipation of the day his wife and children could join him in America. Following the expected VE Day (Victory in Europe) in May the world now turned its attention to the war against the Japanese. America and its Allies gathered their forces for what everyone knew would be a bloody invasion of Japan. However, there would be no invasion. By midsummer news around the world travelled quickly about the United States dropping a ferocious bomb in Hiroshima; but still no surrender from the Japanese. A few days later, a similar, highly destructive bomb destroyed the city of Nagasaki. Hundreds of thousands of Japanese civilians had died. Finally, Japan fell to its knees and unconditional surrender to America and its Allies was agreed upon.

The fall of 1945 saw Massimiliano receive his Honorable Discharge from the United States Army and his letters to my mother further explained how he went back to the business he had left on the Upper East Side of Manhattan. Massimiliano delivered coal and kerosene in the winters and ice in the summers, and he was saving his money for the day his family would be able to travel to America.

That joyful day came in August 1946, when Angela, her daughter Maria and her son Francesco left Naples aboard The Vulcania. After a one day stop-over in Genoa, arrival in New York City would be in eight days.

Tearful goodbyes to her father, step-mother, sisters and the rest of her family at the train station in Bari were softened by the fact that her sister-in-law and brother-in-law, Vincenza (Massimiliano's sister) and Giuseppe accompanied the three US-bound travelers to Naples.

My only memory of the departure from Naples was of being given a large, colorful handkerchief to wave goodbye to my Aunt and Uncle, and my mother crying.

The crossing of the Atlantic was, by all accounts, uneventful, except for my mother constantly yelling at me to stay away from the ship's railing.

I was a few weeks shy of my sixth birthday when we left Italy. My memories of Sannicandro are few, and are as follows:

As a two or three year old, I was always out and about, playing with friends, and almost always barefoot. One day I cut my foot on some glass and I remember crying at the door-step of a neighbor. Another time, I might have been four or five, my friend Vincenzo and I decided to hitch a ride on the back of a mule-driven wagon. The driver didn't take kindly to our adventure and lashed at us with his mule whip. Luckily he missed, but I can still hear the whistling sound of that whip as it whizzed by my ear.

One of my clearest memories occurred when I was taken to Bari for the removal of my tonsils. Because no anesthesia was available I was strapped to a reclining chair with a thick black belt. I remember crying and being promised gelato (ice cream) if I would stop crying.

Two of my older cousins, Frankie and Rocky, introduced me to tobacco. They rolled their own cigarettes and let me take a couple of drags on this homemade cigarette. I don't think I enjoyed it. Another thing these two role models taught me was how to clean myself with a rock after relieving myself in the fields.

The only other memory I have is of women who were screaming and mirrors shaking and then the entire population, or so it seemed, of our town fleeing the village for the relative safety of the countryside. I've been told that this probably occurred the night of June 1943 when British planes bombed our town, killing 95 of our citizens. Subsequent investigations and publications never totally made clear the reason for this attack.

Finally, I have no memories whatsoever of any of my sisters who died, nor was I aware that my father was not with us.

The Crossing

It was a few weeks after my mother, my sister and I arrived in America that my father told us of his illegal crossing of the Atlantic Ocean. Over the years, as I grew into adulthood, he would tell me of his ordeal many times. I can best describe his re-telling as follows:

"We met Salvatore, who was to arrange our illegal boarding of The Rex, the ship that was to transport us to America, in Naples. I was given a crewman's shirt, which was not very comfortable as it was at least two sizes too large for me and the wool fabric was unbearably itchy, but I was told that the section of the ship that would take me and my three fellow stowaways to America would be without heat and we would thank our accomplice for the heavy-duty shirts afterwards. Besides, we had other, more serious concerns, as we listened carefully to the instructions that Salvatore gave us before we were to board the large, ocean-going vessel, the largest of its kind any of us had ever seen.

The plan was to follow Salvatore through the crowd and join the similarly clad men who were hoisting large bundles of supplies onto their shoulders. Once among these men, we were to follow them, bundles on our shoulders, across the gang-plank and to the supply room. After unburdening ourselves of the supplies we were to continue to follow Salvatore, down several steep flights of metal stairways, where he would eventually lead us to a small, unlit closet set in one corner of a large room containing what seemed like miles and miles of white pipes. Once inside the closet, the four of us were to make ourselves as comfortable as possible and wait for Salvatore to come back.

I didn't know the other three men. Two were brothers in their forties and the fourth was someone who introduced himself as Rocco.

I could tell from his dialect that he came from a town very close to my own in southeastern Italy. As the four of us began our introductions, while trying to find some degree of comfort in the tight quarters where we would remain for the next two weeks, it turned out that Rocco was just twenty-five years old, married, and had left his wife with three young children in Grumo, a small town just three miles from Sannicandro, where I had left my wife with four young daughters and a fifth child due later that summer of 1940.

The two brothers were named Vito and Gino and each had left their wives and children behind, hoping to someday have the wherewithal to send for them in America. Their dream was to locate their oldest brother Saverio, who had a successful lumber business in Chicago, and join him in this venture. Hopefully, within the next two or three years they would have saved enough to call for their families to join them. Rumors were going around that the National Origins Act, which had severely restricted the flow of immigrants from southeast Europe almost twenty years earlier, was going to be abolished. However, there were also dark rumors running rampant about Mussolini joining forces with Hitler in his quest to conquer all of Europe before taking on Russia. The future was somewhat foreboding for the four of us seeking our dreams in America, the land of opportunity.

Once settled in the closet, initial introductions concluded, the men grew quiet, each of us lost in his own thoughts. I had ambivalent feelings about leaving my wife Angela with the four girls. The oldest, Meline, was a particular concern for me. She had to be watched at all times. She was eight years old now, but her sisters, Maria, Grazia and Antonia, six, four and two-years old, respectively, were far more advanced than Meline, both physically and mentally.

Unable to speak, incontinent and barely able to walk, she nonetheless had to be restrained almost constantly. We had had a scare the previous summer when Meline became inexplicably separated from us while we were visiting my parents, younger sister and her two young children. In what seemed like a few seconds, we had lost sight of her and alerted the rest of the family, who scattered about the house searching for her.

Our fruitless search carried us outdoors to the backyard and then into the street, where neighbors joined in the search.

Such a calamity had never occurred before. Meline was always within reach, either tethered to her mother, or carried by me. Several hours passed and the search had extended to the entire neighborhood, with no luck. Where could she possibly have gone? All of the neighbors' houses had been searched, back alleys and cellars had been entered, but still no Meline.

It was about ten or eleven o'clock that night, when hope had faded to despair, that word had spread that Meline had been seen in Bitritto, a village about six miles south of Sannicandro. A passing villager, returning from a day's work in the fields on his mule and wagon, had spotted Meline meandering along the only road between the two villages. Realizing immediately that the young girl was retarded and unable to communicate, he was able to put her on the wagon alongside him and brought her to the local church in Bitritto. The nuns there, he figured, would surely know which family she belonged to.

The young nuns the kindly field worker turned Meline over to went immediately to the Mother Superior, who had lived in this village for almost fifty years and knew everyone there by name.

Mother Superior Floretta almost instantly realized that this wayward child, who by now was crying, hungry and had urinated all over herself, came from another village. After tending to Meline's immediate needs, Mother Superior Floretta sent four of the young nuns to the four closest villages to Bitritto to spread the word about Meline's whereabouts. She could only imagine the parents' frantic hours searching for her since her disappearance.

Finally, at just a few minutes past midnight, a local named Luigi had come running into the church to tell Mother Superior that Meline lived with her family in Sannicandro and they were indeed frantic in their efforts to find her. Before the elderly nun could say another word, Angela and I were right behind Luigi and scooped up Meline, who had been tethered to one of the pews in the small church. After thanking her profusely for her kindness, the three of us returned to our village in the borrowed horse and wagon, thankful no harm had come to our severely disabled child.

These were just some of the thoughts running through my head when suddenly the darkened closet door opened and a pail and some left-over food, mostly bread and cheese, with a much too small chunk of salami, were thrown into our eager hands. The pail, Salvatore quickly told us, was for us to relieve ourselves and he would try to come by once a day, if possible, to take the pail from us and bring us some more food. Other amenities, of course, were out of the question. For the next ten days, as the vessel made its way westward toward America, Salvatore would sneak down to us, pick up our "waste basket" and throw some morsels of food to us. Those scraps of food, brought at such irregular intervals, were akin to throwing raw meat to starving wolves.

As the four of us huddled close together in that darkened closet, the passage of time caused our circumstances to become increasingly difficult. We conversed and soon became familiar with all the background information of each man. Information such as wives' and children's names, towns they came from, the type of work they did, what their future plans were upon arrival in America was exchanged. But after what must have been at least five or six days, the conditions under which we had to live took its toll. Unshaven, unwashed and unexercised, our bodies gave off a stench that's best left to the imagination. Surprisingly, however, we reached an understanding as to who and when three of us would sleep, stand and move about while the other curled himself into a corner of the tiny closet that had become our home. We became like brothers on a shared mission; to reach a sort of paradise where brothers, uncles, or cousins would introduce us into a world we knew existed but could only dream about, a world where a man could work eight to ten hours a day, have a decent place to live and eat, and would be able to save enough money so that after a year or two he could send for his wife and children to join him in this wonderful land they called America.

Late one night, perhaps eight or ten days into the crossing, Salvatore came down to tell us they would be docking in New York City early the next morning. He gave each of us a newly-washed and pressed crew member's uniform, which included a cap, and told us to be dressed in it and ready to follow him sometime after sunrise. When Salvatore left us, the fear and anxiety that each man felt was palpable. The possibility of being caught was a real one. Each man knew someone who had had the misfortune to attempt disembarkation in New York City, only to be apprehended by the authorities and sent back to Italy, where a prison sentence awaited him.

It seemed like just a few hours later when a soft knock on the closet door startled us. It was Salvatore, and it was time. America was just up a few flights of stairs and several doors away. Salvatore asked the two brothers, Vito and Gino, to follow him. Before he closed the door on me and Rocco, he assured us he would be right back to fetch us.

Rocco was overcome by anxiety and general nervousness, knowing that very soon he and I would be next to leave that dank and dark closet. He vomited before he could put on the new worker's uniform, which was a blessing of sorts because Rocco's nauseousness seemed to abate somewhat afterwards. After what we thought was about ten days in our "home" we couldn't wait to put on some clean clothing and breathe some fresh air.

As the next few minutes turned into hours, Rocco and I began to worry. Had Salvatore forgotten about us? Had Vito and Gino encountered difficulties in leaving the ship? Almost two weeks of facial growth was sure to be looked upon with suspicion by the authorities. Had the two brothers been caught? Was Salvatore forced to abandon us in that closet? Would the next knock on that closet door be the authorities?

Suddenly, there it was, a soft knock on the closet door. Thankfully, it was Salvatore! At first, we cursed him:

'You told us you'd be right back! Where the hell were you? Did Vito and Gino get off the boat without being caught?'

'Be quiet, you fools!' whispered Salvatore. 'I had to wait until the right time, which is now! So put your hats on and follow me.'

As we made our way up several steep stairways, Salvatore told us to stay right behind him and continue to follow him to the gangplank. When entering the gangplank it was likely that one of the ship's officers would say something to us. Whether that individual spoke to us in English or Italian, we were to keep our heads down, make no eye contact, nod towards the officer by placing a finger on the bill of our cap, and simply mumble, 'yup.'

Rocco and I did exactly as we were told by Salvatore. Sure enough, as we stepped off the ship and onto the gangplank, one of the ship's officers, dressed in the whitest uniform either of us had ever seen, said something to us in English, which neither of us understood. We touched the bill of our caps, mumbled 'yup' and prayed that God was with us as every muscle in our bodies tightened up.

Salvatore was right. We stepped off the gangplank and onto US soil. We continued to follow him through a wooden gate and onto a sidewalk, where the sounds of beeping horns and an unintelligible language was being spoken by numerous men unloading large pieces of luggage onto trucks and carriages.

After walking another fifteen minutes Salvatore turned a corner, led the two us for two more blocks and into a tall, red-brick building. Inside this building, we walked up a short flight of stairs, through still another door, and there we saw Vito and Gino, with huge smiles on their faces.

With a smile none of us had seen on Salvatore's face before, he happily informed us that we were now standing on US soil in the United States of America, in the wonderful city that was called New York, and our hazardous and treacherous journey was almost complete.

The five of us then left the building and went back onto the sidewalk. After another short walk, Salvatore turned, opened a door that led to a long, darkened hallway, walked up three flights of stairs, and rang the doorbell of an apartment. We followed him. As soon as the door was opened, there stood my older brother Nick, smiling. Tears and hugs followed. I was safe; I had made it to America! Nick quickly paid Salvatore the eight hundred dollars for his work, as the other stowaways greeted their respective relatives. In the next few minutes, Nick and I, who hadn't seen each other in almost ten years, left the apartment, bound down the three flights, walked outside, where just a few feet away was Nick's truck. The two of us got into the truck and off to New Jersey we went. I was now officially an illegal resident of America. My heart was pounding so hard I could both feel and hear it inside my chest.

As Nick maneuvered his truck through traffic and south along Twelfth Avenue, he pointed out the river on our right: the mighty Hudson. Before turning into the Lincoln Tunnel, Nick pointed again, this time to a ship that was docked nearby; it was "The Rex," the ship that had brought his younger brother to America.

As we drove towards Newark, Nick told me that he hadn't gotten any mail from Sannicandro in almost a year. Were it not for Salvatore's contacts, he would not have known of my arrival. It had been almost two weeks since I had left Angela and our four children and I couldn't wait to greet Nick's wife Anna and their three young children. More of a priority, however, was my desire for a hot bath and a shave, followed by a hot meal. I had lost much of my girth during my voyage.

But those thoughts faded into the background. My thoughts returned to the present; I was in America now, and the future looked very good. For the first time in many weeks, maybe months, I was smiling."

The Separation

My father's first few months in America were a whirlwind. He reunited with many relatives who had come before him, some legally, like his brother Nick, and some illegally, like himself. After a few weeks, he and another illegal immigrant from Sannicandro found an apartment in Newark, which they shared for several months. My Uncle Nick helped my father get a job working for Lionel model trains, a short distance from their apartment, and in late December 1941, an opportunity to work for himself presented itself when his nephew Jerry, who delivered ice, coal and kerosene out of a cellar on the Upper East Side of Manhattan, was drafted into the Army. My father found an apartment in that neighborhood and thus began a business that would last for more than ten years, minus three very prominent and significant years while he served in the US Army.

My father's US military service came about as a result of President Roosevelt's pronouncement in the aftermath of Pearl Harbor. Citing the need for a large mobilized force upon his declaration of war against Germany, Italy and Japan, the president offered amnesty and US citizenship to illegal aliens willing to serve their new country. My father went on to serve three years as a cook in the US Army. Fortunately, he never served overseas and crisscrossed the country from one coast to the other.

At war's end my father received an honorable discharge and his US Naturalization papers, officially making him a US citizen; both of which were a source of great pride for the remainder of his life.

Meanwhile, the six and a half years that my parents were separated saw my mother experiencing poverty, near starvation and tragedy and finally some degree of prosperity when in 1943 the Allies marched northward up the Italian peninsula. My father, as an active duty American soldier, was then able to send my mother a monthly allotment plus access to the American commissary in nearby Bari.

Finally, less than a year after receiving his honorable discharge, my father was able to reunite with his wife, daughter and the son he had never seen. The six and a half year separation ended on a bright summer day in August 1946 when the four of us embraced. For the next forty-four years my father lived the American dream and punctuated every American holiday and family gathering with a heartfelt "God Bless America!"

Arrival and Assimilation

I always thought I had a pretty good memory, but not remembering two significant events in my life has really bothered me in my later years. My mother, Angela, my older sister, Maria, and I sailed into New York Harbor on August 19, 1946; with the Statue of Liberty on our port side, our ship, The Vulcania, eased its way toward the dock where my father excitedly awaited us, where he would see his wife and daughter for the first time in more than six years, and his soon to be six year old son for the first time. I'd like to retrieve that particular instance from my memory bank from time to time. But no, that's impossible, because I have absolutely no recollection of the two events.

Yes, my mother had told us all about our father; about how he had left in the middle of the night, more than six years earlier, leaving behind a pregnant wife and four young daughters. She told us of his illegal journey across the Atlantic, arriving in America with not a penny in his pocket, but with an older brother who eased his transition those first few difficult and frightening weeks, with immigration officials seemingly lurking around every corner.

She had told us how, after working in factories those first few months, he was able to establish himself in his own business as an iceman in the heart of New York City. And of how he had heeded the American president's call to arms when men were needed to fight the enemy after December 7, 1941; how he had spent more than three years wearing the uniform of the United States Army, had become an American citizen and crisscrossed the country, from New Jersey to Michigan to Colorado to Washington State. She told us that in late 1943, the Allies had advanced northward up the Italian peninsula from Sicily and took control of all of Italy south of Rome. That's when the allotment checks from her GI husband had begun arriving and my mother's life had begun to change, and abject poverty had ceased to be my mother's constant companion. Along with those monthly checks came letters from my father telling us of his life in America. Prior to that, direct communication between my mother and father, from the time he left us in April 1940, until late in 1943, had been sporadic. He wrote of the day that would soon come when the war would be over and he would be able to send for all of us, and he would see his wife, his four daughters and the son he had never seen.

Somewhere in that time frame my mother had to write my father the heartbreaking news of the deaths of three of his daughters, and in all the ensuing years my father never spoke to me of my dead sisters, ever.

My earliest memories after my arrival in America are of my cousin Lina buying me my first pair of American shoes, and a brand new sparkling red tricycle, which was stolen from me just days after its purchase. My twelve year old sister and I were enrolled in St. Stephen's Catholic School, on East 82nd Street, just across the street and down the block from our third floor apartment on First Avenue. Because there were no ESL (English as a Second Language) classes, my sister and I were both placed in a first grade class. As confused and oblivious as I must have been I can imagine how she must have felt sitting in a class with six year olds. It became obvious fairly quickly that we were lost souls when we received disapproving looks from the nun, in her harsh black and white garb as well as from the other students on the day we decided to eat the oranges we had brought to class (perhaps it wasn't lunch hour?)

After a couple of months at St. Stephen's we were transferred to the public school up on Second Avenue. The size of the classes in our new school, we were told, were smaller and would be more conducive to our learning the English language.

At PS 190, I was placed in kindergarten and Mary into sixth grade. Fortunately, I also have no recollection of having major difficulty assimilating, with one possible exception. That occurred when we were asked to bring eggs to class to color them for Easter. The eggs I brought were not hard-boiled and that caused a problem which I'll leave to the imagination.

My promotion to first grade in September 1947 lasted just a month or so when I was "skipped" into second grade. I guess someone noticed that second grade would be more appropriate for someone my age. It was an easy adjustment. The next few years went quickly and I became a regular at the school's after- school and summer playground activities, excelling (at least in my mind) in deck hockey, basketball, ping pong, and softball in the outdoor courtyard. In the neighborhood, stickball, ring-a-lerio, off the point (a form of stoop ball), street football and basketball became my main activities.

All of my teachers at PS 190, Mrs. Plaio in kindergarten, Mrs. Sullivan in first grade, Mrs. Murphy in second grade, Mrs. Ryan, third, Miss Miller, who married and became Mrs. Adler during fourth grade, Mrs. Shortell, in fifth grade, and Mrs. Rigney in sixth grade always gave the same report to my cousin Carmina, who was the official translator for my parents: Frankie should be more serious in class, he's always fooling around. My father, in particular, did not appreciate hearing these comments, and I learned very early that he was a very strict disciplinarian. Fortunately, however, my misbehavior never required a visit to our very stern principal, Miss Novy.

Pretty much all fun and games, though, ended when I graduated from PS 190, and attended PS 30, an all-boys junior high school seven blocks away. The three years, seventh, eighth, and ninth grades at PS 30, which drew a pretty tough crowd from Harlem, were filled mostly by my finding whatever means I could to avoid being beaten up by these tough guys. One memory in particular stands out: A small gang of older boys, probably ninth graders, surrounded me during a visit to the boys' bathroom and took my bag lunch from me. After tossing it in the toilet bowl, they told me that if I still wanted to eat that lunch I'd have to retrieve it from there. I remember one of the boys had a switch blade knife, and when I declined their offer, in tears, they let me go. These boys were pretty tough hombres. My three years at PS 30 were not much fun.

Upon my junior high school graduation in June 1952, I entered Cardinal Hayes High School in the South Bronx, and thus began a three year stint dominated by sports, girls and failing grades.

Destination: America

The years 1880-1924 saw the mass migration of Southern Italians to America. This mass migration, which caused millions of people to leave the land of their birth, was the result of socioeconomic forces which included serious agricultural, educational, economic and political problems. The height of this migration occurred in 1900 when more than six million Italians left for other lands, and most of them came to America, where they were confronted with a different and higher standard of living, a strange and difficult language, unfamiliar customs and laws, and more than occasionally hostile attitudes towards them. However, although the United States Congress passed legislation that severely limited the numbers emigrating from Italy and other Southeastern European countries in 1924, there were still thousands of Italians who somehow found their way across the Atlantic. This memoir is about both sides of my family, my mother's side and my father's side, and the manner in which they made their way to America. The sacrifices that these men and women made amaze me every time I think about it. Let me begin with my father's side first:

My father, Massimiliano, had two older brothers, Vincenzo and Nicola, and one younger sister, Vincenza.

My father's father, Francesco, and oldest brother Vincenzo arrived in America, through Ellis Island, in 1914. As described in a separate memoir, Vincenzo's time here was cut short when he was drafted into the Italian Army, and he was killed in action in 1915. My father's next oldest sibling, Nick, traveled to America by himself, in 1920, when he was nineteen years old. He had friends in Chicago and he settled there for several years. In 1928, Nick returned to his home in Sannicandro, a small village on the outskirts of Bari, a port city on the Adriatic Sea. There he met and married Anna Clarizio and the newlyweds set off for America together. Rather than return to Chicago, Anna and Nick settled in New Jersey, where Anna's three brothers had established businesses and allowed Nick to join them.

In 1933, Anna, Nick and their two young daughters, Mary and Jean (Maria and Vincenza) returned to Italy, where they intended to rejoin their parents and remain. However, Naziism and Fascism began their encroachment throughout Europe, bringing with them the dark clouds of World War II. Heeding the advice of their parents, Anna and Nick, along with their daughters, returned to America, and settled in New Jersey, where Nick established himself as a successful businessman for the next fifty-four years. It was Nick's success, as well as his contacts that forged the way, years later, for his younger brother and sister to find their way to the United States.

In 1940, my father, Massimiliano, 31, married and the father of four young girls left his pregnant wife and made his way to America as a stowaway. Fortunately, his brother, Nick, who had been living in the states for almost twenty years, was able to ease his younger brother's adjustment to life as an illegal immigrant. Massimiliano was not to see his family again until 1946.

The more than six year separation was not without sacrifice, deprivation and loss for my father. My parents suffered through tremendous loss; and of his four daughters, the oldest, Maria Carmela, was developmentally disabled and required round the clock care. Five months after his departure, his fifth child and first son, Francesco, was born. Three months later, his two younger daughters, Grazia and Antonia, died three weeks apart --one from pneumonia, the other typhus. They were two and four years old, respectively. Three years later, a third child, the oldest, Maria Carmela, passed at the age of thirteen. As recounted in a previous, detailed episode, these difficult times were borne by my mother without the support of my father or her own mother, who had died when my mother was nine years old.

Meanwhile, in America, Massimiliano was able to elude the immigration authorities and established himself in Manhattan, where he operated an ice, coal and kerosene delivery business. December 7, 1941, brought significant changes to millions around the world. To Massimiliano, it meant the opportunity to serve in the United States Army. America's President, Franklin D. Roosevelt, citing the need for mobilization of a large army when war was declared against Japan, Germany and Italy, promised both amnesty and citizenship to illegal aliens willing to serve in America's armed services. Although he was a veteran of Mussolini's army and had served in North Africa in the early 1930's, Massimiliano saw FDR's offer as a great opportunity for him and his family. After serving as a private first class and a cook for three years in the US Army, his decision to serve paid dividends upon the conclusion of the war when he received both his US citizenship and his honorable discharge from the army and was able to bring his wife Angela, daughter Maria and son Francesco to join him in his adopted country. It was a decision he never regretted.

Nick and Masy's younger sister, Vincenza, traveled a different path in her journey to America. Married to Giuseppe in 1936, she was the mother of two children, a daughter, Rosella, three, and an infant son Giovanni when, in 1940, her husband was drafted into the Italian Army. Shortly afterwards, Giuseppe was on a troop ship destined for North Africa when it was torpedoed and sunk. After twenty-four harrowing hours clinging to some flotsam in the Mediterranean Sea, he was picked up by a British ship and served the remainder of the global conflict as a Prisoner of War, courtesy of the British. Much of that time was spent in sordid conditions in South Africa, and his family had no information as to whether he had survived the sinking of his ship.

At war's end, in 1945, Giuseppe returned home, had another child, a son, Francesco, and proceeded to struggle to support them on the meager living he was able to extract from the land. In 1951, unable to secure passage to America, he made his way to Venezuela, where many of his countrymen had gone to seek employment and opportunity that was unavailable in their native land. After establishing himself outside Caracas, working as a ranch hand, he sought to have his wife and three children join him there. His wife, however, was reluctant to leave her elderly, widowed father, and so they remained apart until their older son, Giovanni, turned eighteen, in 1958, and went to Venezuela to join his father. The two men lived and worked there for the next seven years. Meanwhile, the oldest child, Rosella, was able to secure passage to America under the quota system; the year was 1959 and she was twenty-one years old. During those five years Rosella lived with her Uncle Massimiliano and her Aunt Angela and their three children. And so for the next five years these five family members, husband Giuseppe, wife Vincenza, two sons, and one daughter lived on three different continents. Rosella lived with her Uncle Massimiliano and his family until 1964, and shortly after becoming a US citizen was able to have her mother and grandfather join her. It was her grandfather's fourth and final journey to America. His first three trips are recounted in a separate episode.

As it turned out, 1964 was a good year for this family: In addition to Vincenza and her elderly father (he was ninety-five at the time) joining their daughter in America, Giuseppe and his oldest son Giovanni were permitted to leave Venezuela and join them. A few weeks later, the youngest son, Francesco, arrived, and the family, for the first time in almost fifteen years, was together.

The three siblings' journey to America was a long and winding one, but they endured, survived and, ultimately, thrived. God Bless America!

And now for my mother's side of the story: My mother was the youngest of three sisters. Her oldest sister, Catherine, was married with two children, Gennaro (Jerry) and Maria when, in 1930, just prior to the birth of her third and youngest child, Angelantonio (Tony), her husband, Nick, traveled to America, where he became involved in several businesses. Included among these were an Italian restaurant and a candy store. His oldest son was able to join him in the mid-thirties, and his wife and two other children followed several years after the end of the Second World War. As it happened, my Uncle Nick and his youngest son, Tony, did not meet until Tony was sixteen years old!

My mother's middle sister, Donata, and her husband, my Uncle Luigi, chose a different manner in their quest to come to America. Uncle

Luigi, prior to his marriage, made several treks to this country, each time staying a year or two and making enough money to be able to go back to his home town in Italy and help his family financially. He and Aunt Donata married after he returned from his third trip here and proceeded to have seven children. Each of their children's stories is interesting in their own right, but suffice it to say that two of the children, Francesco and Rosalie and their spouses and children chose to remain in Italy for various reasons. The other five, Angelantonio (Tony), Vito, Rocco, Maria and Angela (Lina) arrived at different times. The second oldest, Vito, arrived as a stowaway after the conclusion of WWII; my aunt and uncle arrived ten years later, courtesy of the fact that Vito became a naturalized citizen and was allowed to bring them here legally. Three years after their arrival, their three youngest children, Rocco, Maria, and Lina, who had remained in Italy in the intervening three years living with their oldest brother and his wife and children, finally arrived in America.

Finally, in 1970, at the age of 43, Aunt Donata and Uncle Luigi's oldest child, Tony, arrived in America with his wife Rosa and three young sons.

I can't emphasize enough how much these families sacrificed, all for the opportunity to live in this great country of ours. My families' story has been repeated millions of times, both in years past, and continues to this day, by people from around the globe. Amazing!

The Cellar

The cellar was about ten or twelve steps below the sidewalk, and was just a few feet off First Avenue on 82nd Street in Manhattan. It was where my father's workplace, his "office," if you will, was located. He sold ice, coal and kerosene to the tenants and small businesses on that block between First and Second Avenues. It was a one-man operation, except for those cold winter days when he told me I had to sit down there and take customers' orders while he made his deliveries. For all the help I provided, I would say that on those days it became a one and a quarter man operation, as I was just nine or ten years old at the time and didn't really do very much.

In the summertime, when he sold only ice for the saloons and tenants' ice boxes, he closed the steel double doors of the cellar, and kept his large blocks of ice against the building, in the shade. He covered the ice with burlap bags to slow the melting process. Alongside these blocks of ice were his wooden push cart, ice pick and ice tongs. When my father had to cut a twenty-five or fifty cent piece of ice from the large block, that ice pick and those tongs became magic wands in his hands. He was like a skilled surgeon with those tools. He knew exactly the right size for each price; he would first score the ice with the tongs, and then use the ice pick to chop the rest of the way through. Then he clutched the piece between the tongs and placed it at an angle in the tub so that it didn't go all the way into the tub. Amazingly, the cuts he made were always neat and precise. He would then fold a burlap bag several times, place it on one of his shoulders, and hoist the tub of ice onto his shoulder. The burlap prevented the tub from digging into his shoulder. None of the apartment buildings had elevators so if Mrs. Melchionno or Mrs. O'Riley lived on the fourth or fifth floor, he would climb those steps with that tub of ice or bag of coal on his shoulder. My father was a very strong man.

In the winters he would store coal and several large barrels of kerosene in the cellar. He would deliver forty to fifty pound bags of coal, five gallon cans of kerosene, and blocks of ice to his customers throughout the day. Since his "office" had no phone, people would place their orders by shouting down from the top step of the cellar to my father's assistant (me) below. Until the customers realized who it was that was taking their delivery orders, the routine went something like this:

"Hey, Sonny, is Jerry there?" ("Jerry" was the previous owner's name and that's what all the customers called him.)

"No, he's out on a delivery. Can I help you?"

"Yeah…are you Jerry's son?"

"Yes I am."

"What's yer name, kid?"

"Frankie."

"Okay, Frankie, tell yer father to deliver a fifty cent block of ice to Mrs. Melchionno at # 330, apartment 3A."

"OK."

Then I went back to my chair, which was placed directly in front of the kerosene stove that kept me warm those long winter days. I hated being there, but realized I had no choice. As my father's only son, I became the chosen one.

From the time I was about nine or ten years old, taking those kinds of messages pretty much constituted the bulk of the duties my father assigned to me. It was 1948 or '49, and most people on the Upper East Side of Manhattan still had ice boxes to keep their food and liquids cold.

The cellar consisted of a small area where, in the winter, my father and I huddled over a kerosene stove in order to keep warm while waiting for business to develop. Adjacent to this area was a small room where the kerosene barrels were stored. Some of my father's customers brought the empty cans and asked to have them filled so they could bring them to their apartments themselves. I did the filling. Unfortunately, this task was so quick and simple that there was never any tip when I handed the full can to the customer.

The five gallon cans of kerosene, the twenty-five and fifty cent blocks of ice, and the forty and fifty pound bags of coal were simply too heavy for me, so I manned the "office" while my father made his deliveries. Occasionally, a customer would want a two gallon can of kerosene delivered and I looked forward to making those deliveries myself for two reasons: First, it gave me the chance to leave the drudgery and cold of the cellar, and, second, I often received a tip, which I promptly spent on a candy bar at Jenny's candy store, located on 83rd Street. "Good and Plenty" and "Hollywood" candy bars were my favorites. I bought those candy bars and gobbled them down on the way back to the cellar, unbeknownst to my father.

There was a large, dimly lit area in the back of this cellar. On one side there was a cold water faucet and a sink, and the other side was where the coal was stored. When the week or month's supply of coal was delivered, the supply truck backed onto the sidewalk, and then extended a long, metal slide that slid the coal all the way to the back where the coal was to be stored. I'll always remember the extremely loud, grating noise and the dark cloud of dust that that process produced. The back area that had the faucet and sink was used on occasion by my father to slaughter rabbits that were to serve as our Easter holiday dinner. I distinctly remember spending very little time in those two back areas.

I probably worked in the cellar until I was twelve or thirteen, or until my father sold the business in the early fifties. The advent of the refrigerator was the beginning of the end for the ice men. I rarely worked in the cellar in the summer because there was little or no need to heat apartments either with kerosene or with coal, so most of my working hours took place in the winters. I remember huddling around the kerosene stove shivering, smelling like kerosene and dreaming of better days ahead.

I hated working in the cellar. Whenever I could find a reason, any reason at all, to excuse myself from working down there I took advantage of it. My father knew I didn't want to be there and was rarely pleasant when we were there together. My negative vibes probably rubbed off on him. I remember once asking him why he didn't ever pay me, not once, not a penny, for all the cold winter hours I spent in the cellar, and I'll always remember his reply.

"Do you see that food that you're eating at home every day? Well, that's your pay."

I disagreed with his payment policy, but I knew there was no point in arguing.

Many years later, when I had a son of my own, I asked him to do odd jobs around my property. After he finished mowing the lawn or raking leaves, I remember over-reacting to my father's stinginess by over-paying my son. Maybe I should have barbecued him a couple of hot dogs instead.

Kennel Master

Dr. Robert Sterling was his name, and he and his brother Oscar ran a highly successful dog and cat hospital on the Upper East Side of Manhattan. The two-story building which housed this commercial establishment was located on the northwest corner of 83d Street and First Avenue. The structure was painted white on the outside, and one could usually hear the sounds of animals yapping emanating from inside its walls at all hours of the day. Its clients were mostly well-to-do professionals: businessmen, professional athletes, and even some Hollywood actors; Basil Rathbone was known to be among this elite clientele.

There was only one problem with which Dr. Sterling and brother Oscar had to contend in their thriving endeavor, and that was the group of young boys who played stickball and off the point, two variations of the game of baseball, with a Spaldeen, a pinkish, hollow rubber ball substituting for an actual baseball. These young lads played their games across the street from their place of business, and the Spaldeen often found its way smashing through the good doctor's windows. On those all too often occurrences this group of young boys scattered and were nowhere to be found so as to be held accountable for their misdeeds.

However, those escapes from the clutches of this successful veterinarian would not continue forever. Somehow, among these young boys, ranging in age from twelve to fifteen, and whose names were Chuckie, Tommy, Vernie, Mikie, Johnny, Ronnie, Tony, Ray, and Frankie, it was yours truly, the last named, whom Dr. Sterling fingered one hot summer day.

There were five or six of us that day, just hanging around, enjoying cold bottles of Coke; we were inactive due to Ray's prodigious feat of the previous day whereby he hit the ball over the building and onto the roof of the dog and cat hospital. Until we could muster up the two-bits a brand new Spaldeen would cost us, we spent the time discussing our local baseball heroes: Willie, Mickey, and the Duke, or sometimes it was Pee Wee or Phil "the Scooter" Rizzuto.

As we were arguing the relative merits of these baseball gods, Dr. Sterling ambled over to our group, looked directly at me, and asked if he could speak to me privately. I think he chose me because I was leading our group in broken windows. At any rate, the good doctor asked if I'd be willing to make a couple of dollars a week by working as an assistant in his office. I guess he figured that if I was working in his office, I couldn't be outside hitting balls through his windows. Well, two dollars a week to a thirteen year old kid in 1953 could buy an awful lot of Cokes and Spaldeens. Without asking too many questions I eagerly accepted his offer. And thus began my experiences with animals, dogs in particular, which would provide memories that would last a lifetime.

My duties as the veterinarian's assistant included answering the phone, processing the paperwork, and sometimes taking the dogs from their owners and placing them in cages, where they would be boarded for up to several days at a time. And because this was a professional environment I had to wear a suit, the only suit I owned. I worked only on Saturdays, from 9 AM till 1 PM, and my salary was fifty cents an hour, for a grand total of two dollars, off the books. The thought of those two bucks a week made my mouth water.

My employment at the hospital lasted just a month or two, as I recall, and two memories in particular remain vivid:

The first occurred when Dr. Sterling asked if I would like to assist his brother Oscar with a surgical procedure that was to take place on a Saturday evening. It was to last for about two hours and I would be paid seventy five cents per hour. Again, without asking any questions, I eagerly accepted the offer.

The surgical procedure involved Oscar's clipping or shortening the tail and ear flaps of a dog that I think was a Boxer. The evening went reasonably well, and though Oscar had the disheveled appearance of a stereotypical mad scientist, with wild, unruly hair, thick glasses and a wild-eyed gaze that made me more than a bit uncomfortable, he apparently knew what he was doing, and my assistance as his "go-fer" satisfied him. The procedure that evening was relatively bloodless and my duties consisted of handing him various instruments and other utensils essential to the task. At evening's end, I collected my buck-fifty for the night's work, and felt proud of my accomplishment, such as it was.

The other memory is less pleasant and resulted in my leaving the employ of the good doctor. It occurred one Saturday morning while I was walking a Dachshund, or "Frankfurter" dog, which was the vernacular used to describe the long-trunked and short-legged creature. The cage that was to be its "home" for the immediate future was on the upper level of cages and required my picking up the animal and placing him in the cage.

What you may not know about me is the fact that I had never owned a dog and was in fact afraid of the four legged critters, and so lifting this warm, living, moving animal was awkward, to say the least. However, as I endeavored to perform my duty, and just as I had her at shoulder level and about to push her into the cage, I felt a warm wetness running down my neck and back. This "adorable" pet had peed all over me, and worse, all over my one and only suit! Absolutely disgusted, I pushed her into the cage, locked the door, and went into Dr. Sterling's office.

The look on my face, as well as the smell emanating from me, required no explanation. Seeming somewhat annoyed, Dr. Sterling told me my work-day was finished, and he would see me the following Saturday. When I arrived home, my mother and father were not very pleased at the condition of my suit jacket, told me to return to the hospital to collect my pay for the day's work, and also to inform Dr. Sterling that my days as a veterinarian's assistant were finished.

PS – There are many reasons why I have never owned a dog, but foremost among them is the fact that I can still feel and smell that Frankfurter dog's urine all over me!

PPS – My family and I moved away from that Upper East Side neighborhood when I was sixteen, and several times over the years

I returned and stood at the spot where I launched all those Spaldeen balls against that white dog and cat hospital, or smashed them through its windows. The two story building was razed some years later to make room for a high rise, but when I go back there every now and then I can still see Dr. Sterling in his white coat, running out of his office and yelling at that group of kids who had just broken another window.

My First Date

I was sixteen when I had my first date. The girl's name was Regina and we had met at Randall's Island, where a few of my friends and I had biked several times that summer of 1957; we went there to play baseball. We lived in Astoria and it wasn't too bad of a ride. Although one of our excursions resulted in my crashing my friend's bicycle and winding up in a hospital emergency room (see separate memoir), all of the other times we went there we had a pretty good time.

My friends from Astoria were Vito, Freddie, Tony and a few others whose names I can't remember. Luckily for us, we didn't play too much baseball because some girls from the South Bronx had walked over the Triboro Bridge to picnic in the same area. We got along pretty well with the girls and I had my eye on a cute brunette with a very nice smile. She seemed to like me too, and so I was thrilled when she said yes when I asked her out on a date; I was sixteen and Regina would be my first date!

I had to take two separate trains from my house in Astoria to get to her house in the Bronx. I remember being very nervous as I approached her apartment building, where Regina lived with her mother. All I remember about the evening was that we went to a movie, and the entire time we were sitting together I was trying to figure out when and how to put my arm over and around her shoulders. The movie was probably half over before I got the nerve to first remove my right arm from the armrest. Then, slowly, gradually, and ever so cautiously, I maneuvered my arm across the back of her seat, and draped my arm and hand over her shoulder. I was very careful not to brush her neck because it might startle her. I remember feeling very apprehensive about this process, fearing she might move away from me, or say something about my aggressive move. Since this was the first time I had ever had my arm or any part of my body for that matter so close to a girl, I wasn't quite sure what I was doing or where I should stop. I'm not sure how long this particular position of my arm and hand lasted, but I do remember that I became very uncomfortable and my right arm started to tingle and fall asleep. I know that I didn't want to move my hand because I wanted the feeling of my hand draped over her shoulder to last as long as possible. Regina must have liked it too because she never made a move indicating I was being too aggressive. However, my arm was starting to tingle worse than ever and I became very uncomfortable.

I guess the movie was coming to an end when all of a sudden Regina shifted her body on the seat and moved her right arm, which I saw as an opportunity to bring my arm back to my side. At that point I wasn't quite sure what I should do. The tingling sensation had stopped, so I held her hand for the remainder of the movie, feeling a little bit proud of how I handled myself.

When I walked her home that evening I gave Regina a quick and awkward goodnight kiss and headed home. The next time I saw her was at a party and my fickle and wandering eye was immediately drawn to one of her friends, Evelyn, with whom I began a short and ultimately heart-breaking relationship. I kind of ignored Regina a couple of other times I saw her and heard from her friends that she still liked me, but as I said my heart was with Evelyn.

Over the years, I've thought of Regina and our one and only date which for me was my very first date. She was such a nice girl and I'm sure she got over me. But hopefully, if she reads my book, she'll have fond memories of me as I do of her.

Where Are the Girls?

I attended Junior High School # 30 in Manhattan, where I spent grades seven, eight and nine. It was a single sex school; that means there were no girls. For a post-pubescent boy it meant that my learning curve regarding the birds and bees would have to wait or simply lie dormant.

By the time I was ready to transfer to a high school, where I would spend grades ten, eleven and twelve, another three years, it was decided by my parents that I would attend Cardinal Hayes High School in the South Bronx. That was fine with me, until I learned that it too was a single sex school. So, for another three years, a time during which one would expect a young virile male such as myself to learn quite a bit about those birds and bees, I learned practically nothing. Oh, yes, there were the occasional mixers, hovered over by Catholic priests and brothers and nuns. But they didn't lend themselves to very much learning in that field of endeavor which occupied my every waking minute.

So, by the time I graduated from high school, all of seventeen years old, with no sexual experience of any kind, and totally lacking in self-confidence, with no college acceptance letters addressed to me, I entered the world of business. I was able to land a job at Best & Co., an upscale department store in Manhattan. I started as a stock-boy, and after a couple of months, I became an elevator operator. Finally, there were girls, hundreds of them: there were stock girls, sales girls, secretaries, hair stylists, and plenty of young female customers. The only problem was that I was painfully shy. Although I was able to mumble my way into a few dates, my lack of encounters with young girls resulted in very awkward experiences.

Shortly after I turned eighteen, in September of 1958, I joined the United States Air Force where, for the next four years, my interactions with females once again were limited. Oh, I had some encounters, and I can't call them relationships because they never developed to a point where I could describe them as that. After seven months in Texas, I was reassigned to Lockbourne Air Force Base, just outside Columbus, Ohio. It was in Ohio that I began to learn about those elusive birds and bees. But lo and behold, after just fifteen months of acquainting myself with those creatures, I was reassigned once again, this time to Alaska, where females were once again a rare commodity. And so for the remainder of my four year enlistment, for the next twenty-two months in that cold outpost, girls once again were beyond my eager reach.

Ah, but times, and my life, would change. In July of 1962, I received my honorable discharge from the Air Force and I began college that fall....at a co-ed college. And so, after ten long years of extremely limited contact with half the world's population, I was ready to live life as a normal young American male, and I feasted!

Cardinal Hayes

"Rise and shine, bow-tie Charlie, rise and shine!"

That is how I was addressed many times in my World History class. Father McCormick loved to tag his students with nicknames, and my mother's insistence that I wear a bow tie singled me out rather easily by the needling priest.

I spent grades ten, eleven and twelve of my high school years at a Catholic institution called Cardinal Hayes, which was located on the Grand Concourse in the South Bronx. The all-boys high school required, among other essentials, that a jacket and tie be worn at all times. I think I wore the same jacket and a couple of ties for all three years.

As a junior high school and elementary school student, I was always fooling around, and despite my many antics, I was able to get decent grades. However, once I entered Hayes as a tenth grader, my shenanigans and monomaniacal musings on sports and girls resulted in failing grades from the very beginning. I guess the worst class for me was German. Although I had done B and B+ work in both seventh and eighth grade German, I think that I should have been placed in a second year high school level German class, but instead I was placed in a third year course, with a Regents exam looming at its conclusion. From the first day of that class to the very end, ten months later, I basically felt lost. I failed both the course and the Regents exam. The teacher, a most intimidating man of the cloth, was, in hindsight, not at all discerning of the fact that I should have been moved to a second year level. The fact that on more than one occasion a mischievous student incurred Brother's wrath and the physical beatings that followed did not in any way encourage me to speak out about my frustrations in the course.

In the three years I spent at Hayes I witnessed several instances where a teacher (a priest or a brother) would resort to inflicting corporal punishment on some poor unsuspecting young man. The action that caused these physical confrontations was unknown to me, and so whether or not they were warranted I'll never know.

My lackluster performance in the German class meant that I had to attend summer school, which I did. The edifice whose presence I graced was Washington Irving High School in lower Manhattan; it was the summer of 1956. August saw me failing both the course and the Regents once again, and that marked the end of my Germanic studies. As I reflect back, I wonder if it was really necessary that I attend summer school. Since I never did receive credit for the course, and I still received my diploma two years later, I think not.

During all of my sophomore year, my quarterly report cards showed that I was also failing Religion and World History. How I received a final passing grade in Religion I'll never know, but I did. As for World History, because I passed the Regents exam, I was given a final passing grade of 65.

Junior year passed with the same results. In that year, Bookkeeping, Religion and American History were my nemeses. I also remember that both my music teacher and English teacher, both Catholic priests, inflicted physical punishment on a couple of misbehaving youngsters. And Washington Irving once again became my summer school of choice. That was 1957, the course was Bookkeeping, but the result was different: I received a final summer school grade of 95. I should have brought that report card to the Brother who failed me, but that would've probably resulted in a swift backward hand across my face, so I'm glad I didn't do it.

I might add that after my sophomore year, I was advised to discontinue taking the elective academic courses that were considered college preparatory, and to focus instead on a Commercial course of studies. In fact, in the Typing, Shorthand and Transcription courses in which I was enrolled in both my Junior and Senior years, I excelled!

My three years at Hayes were interspersed with attempts on my part to participate in interscholastic sports. My try-outs with the varsity baseball and basketball teams proved fruitless, but I did continue with my basketball pursuits by participating in Hayes' intramural basketball program after school hours. To my eternal regret I learned that both Bob Cousy's and Mickey Mantle's jobs on their respective championship teams were not in any jeopardy.

While on the subject of the occasional physical beatings I witnessed at Hayes, the one priest who was probably the most intimidating figure in the entire school was a gentleman who held the title of Dean of Discipline. This man patrolled the halls and occasionally entered a classroom, whereupon the entire class was required to stand upon his entrance. If he wasn't pleased with the length of one's hair or the disheveled appearance of a student he would invariably call that young man to the front of the room and verbally assault him, demanding that the wayward student amend his ways. The Dean's final statement to the student was almost always, "Tomorrow, young man, your mother will be in my office first thing in the morning!" His six-foot four inch physical bearing meant that the offending student would never, ever, utter a word of defiance, lest the Dean ravage him. Thankfully, I was never the target of his attacks.

June 22, 1958 finally arrived and I received my high school diploma in an emotional graduation ceremony held at St. Patrick's Cathedral in New York City. A few months later, I found myself committed to Uncle Sam for four years, four years that I needed in order to understand the discipline, focus and diligence needed to succeed at the college level. And four years after that, I received my Bachelor's degree from Albany State University, and a few years after that accomplishment I received my Master's Degree in Counseling, facts that I'm sure would shock many of the brothers and priests at Cardinal Hayes High School.

Frank John Tassielli

"Frankie" . . . Precious Blood
. . . Business Club 3, 4 . . .
Class Basketball 2, 3, 4 . . .
Class Vice President 1 . . .
plans to attend C.C.N.Y. for
Business . . . likes Typing.

High School Yearbook

Best & Co.

"Second floor, ladies' furs. Going up? Yes, ma'am. Watch your step, please."

"Third floor, ladies' lingerie. Going up? Yes, ma'am. Please watch your step."

"Fourth floor, children's furniture. Going up? Yes, sir. Watch your step, please."

And so it went, up, down, up, down, up, down....

My career at Best & Co. began when I was a senior in high school. I worked part-time as a stock boy until I graduated. Since college was not an option at that point in my life, and unable to find any other suitable employment, I went back to Best that summer. I was always partial to the color blue, so when I turned eighteen at summer's end and was offered a blue uniform, which was the uniform that Best's elevator operators wore and came with a ten dollar a week raise, I accepted immediately. Best & Co. was an upscale department store located on 51st and Fifth Avenue in New York City. And so for the next couple of months I went absolutely nowhere, and the monotony soon engulfed me.

Those two months, however, were filled with experiences that helped me in other ways. Young salesgirls, stock girls, and female customers seemed to notice the effect the blue uniform had on me, and numerous encounters introduced me to the world of love and romance. There were many employees who were in the same age bracket as I and so I was able to make many friends, some platonic, some not.

I became an automaton over the next few weeks as those elevators insisted on making the same ten stops every single time, up, down, up, down. No sideways, no new floors, same faces, same smiles; it was getting to me. One day in October the color blue grabbed me again when the United States Air Force, with its dark blue uniform, won me over, and I signed up for a four year commitment, hoping the structure and discipline would benefit me. Well, four years of Air Force duty later and upon my honorable discharge from military service at the age of twenty-two, it was déjà vu all over again as I once more donned the blue uniform of Best & Co.'s elevator operators. Up, down, up, down; for the next two years I did this every Saturday and many holidays when I had no classes at the community college I was attending on a full-time basis. And once again, to my delight, the salesgirls and stock girls were everywhere. My salary actually remained the same as it was when I was just out of high school, but my maturity and self-awareness made my experience at Best more fruitful.

One of the more memorable experiences I had while working at Best occurred on a Christmas Eve. After leaving work in the early evening, my friend Doreen and I decided to attend Christmas Eve Mass at St. Patrick's Cathedral, which was just a few steps from Best. Upon leaving the church, we encountered a blind, elderly man who was having difficulty traversing the steps leading out to the street. Besides his cane, he was also carrying a black suitcase. In our eagerness to assist this man, I offered to carry his suitcase while Doreen offered to walk him home, which was just a few blocks away. It was Christmas Eve, after all. What I didn't realize was how heavy the suitcase was, and also what the gentleman meant by "just a few blocks." What was in that suitcase, I wondered, as I lagged behind Doreen and our new friend? Why was it so heavy? And how far is it to his apartment building? After almost an hour of walking south on Fifth Avenue, and then several blocks west to his residence, I was relieved when we finally stopped at his front door because I would finally be able to return the suitcase, which by now felt like it weighed a ton, to the blind man. Our good deed was not quite over, however. As he thanked us for our Christian goodness, and bade us a Merry Christmas, he opened his suitcase, which revealed bottles filled with hairsprays and shampoos and hair conditioners, and tried to sell us some. We respectfully declined and finally made our way home to spend the remainder of our Christmas Eve with our families. I said goodbye to Doreen and thanked her for her graciousness in helping the blind man.

That was but one of many memories that I have from my employment with Best & Co.

Four Years with Uncle Sam

"Shape up, airman! You'd better have your shoes and belt buckle shining so I can see my face in it! If you don't, you won't make it out of basic training and we'll send you back home to your mama!"

Master Sergeant Terry, the highest ranking NCO in my squadron, was eyeball to eyeball with me as I stood, ramrod straight, and listened, with my knees buckling, to his reprimand.

"Yes, sir," I responded, in the most assertive voice I could muster. Inwardly, I felt about six inches tall as the First Sergeant continued his harangue.

How in the world did I get myself into this situation? Less than a week earlier I had been an elevator operator at Best & Co. I was earning fifty bucks a week and hadn't a care in the world. Then, seduced by the grand promises of the recruiting sergeant, I had raised my right hand and swore to serve my country faithfully for four years. At that point in my life I thought I was about to embark on an adventure that would take me to distant and exotic lands around the world. Little did I know that these exciting travels hinged on my ability to expertly spit shine my shoes and belt buckle. I had a lot to learn.

Somehow, though, I did become expert at this task, as well as a few others, such as mopping floors, scrubbing pots and pans, and marching. Boy, did I learn how to march! From the very first day of basic training, we marched and marched and marched, from one end of Lackland Air Force Base in south Texas to the other, and back. With split-second efficiency, we responded to commands such as, "Left oblique, march!" "About face, march!" "Double-time, march!" Oh, and almost as an after-thought, our leaders remembered that we were soldiers, and taught us how to fire an M-1, the standard-issue weapon for enlisted Air Force personnel in the late 1950's. Not one single weapon of any kind, other than the M-1, was ever introduced to us.

Ultimately, I became skilled enough to earn three stripes during my four year enlistment. Unfortunately, however, when my basic training ended, I had hoped I would be reassigned to a different base and see some other part of our country. Instead, I was sent to the other side of Lackland AFB, where I would train to become an Air Force Personnel Specialist, which, translated into civilian jargon, means a clerk typist. I spent the next seven months there, and got to see quite a bit of beautiful downtown San Antonio. When my training ended, my hoped-for exotic adventures were delayed once again when I was assigned to Lockbourne AFB, just outside Columbus, Ohio, where I would spend the next fifteen months. That assignment was followed by a lengthy tour at Elmendorf AFB, which was located just three miles from Anchorage, Alaska, not exactly what I had been led to expect by the recruiting sergeant who convinced me to sign the dotted line and become government property for forty-eight months.

However, as I look back on my experience with the Air Force, I know now, and have known for some time, that it really was one of the best decisions I ever made. A major reason it was such a fortuitous and fateful decision was that my four years of active duty occurred after the Korean Conflict had ended and before the Vietnam War had begun. Two other reasons were that the four years were a time that I needed to grow up, learn some self-discipline, and realize the value of a college education, something my mother was unsuccessful in conveying to me during my high school years. And speaking of family, those four years, and living far from home, gave me a much-needed perspective and taught me the value of family.

As an eighteen year old just out of high school, going up and down in that elevator, I had truly been a lost soul. I didn't know who I was, nor did I know where I was going, or how I was going to get there. That recruiting sergeant who approached me as I emerged from the East 86th Street subway station knew he had me hooked as I glared, open-mouthed, at his shiny blue uniform with a chest full of medals. His promises of exciting and romantic times with beautiful female creatures from distant lands who would be attracted by young and handsome soldiers, sailors and airmen had me begging to sign the enlistment papers. An additional allure was his comment that the Air Force could also train me to become a jet plane mechanic. Visions of a long and successful career as a master mechanic for TWA or United Airlines, earning a salary that would dwarf my pay as an elevator jockey were swirling around in my mind. For the most part, however, those tantalizing thoughts proved fruitless.

My first week in basic training in Texas taught me not only how to spit shine my shoes and belt-buckle, it also taught me that the battery of tests I took showed I had little or no mechanical ability. Remember, I didn't know who I was. But I was learning.

Yes, I was learning. Here are a few other things I learned:

Prior to our being given orders as to where we would be assigned upon completion of our Personnel Specialist program at Lackland, I was called into one of our sergeant's office, where he proceeded to lead me into a nearby latrine. There he informed me that I was going to be shipped to either the outer reaches of northern North Dakota, or the middle of the prairie in Kansas. However, if I slipped him forty dollars he would arrange it so I would be assigned to a base in Maine, a few hours' drive from my home. Stunned by his proposal, I declined, and walked out, and later that day, my orders read "Lockbourne Air Force Base," outside Columbus, Ohio. Go figure.

My time in Ohio was pretty interesting. I learned quite a bit about life and love. Cupid paid me his first visit; her name was Maxine and she was sixteen and I was eighteen, and I thought my future with her and the entire world lay at my feet. After all, we were in love! Or so I thought. A few short weeks after our mutual declaration of everlasting love, her father, a master sergeant on the base, was reassigned, along with his family, to England.

My time in Ohio ended when I was summoned by my commanding officer. He told me that a few of us in the squadron were being shipped overseas. Once again, my teenaged hormones conjured up images of scantily clad native girls in hula skirts, dancing on the sun-drenched beaches of some South Pacific island, waving for me to join them. My sex-obsessed nineteen year old brain was jolted back to reality when Captain Winters informed me that I had a choice, and asked for no cash, mind you! I could either spend the next thirteen months in Korea, or the next twenty-four months in Alaska. I remember thinking, "What kind of choice is this he's offering me!" Neither assignment thrilled me. Before I could answer, he received a phone call from headquarters informing him that in fact I had no choice at all. Elmendorf Air Force Base, just outside Anchorage, Alaska, would indeed be my home for the next two years. He added with a snide grin that although the Eskimos would surely keep me warm, I should also pack some extra sweaters and galoshes.

My time in Alaska was in fact interesting because of the many good friendships I formed, a couple of which last to this day, more than fifty years later. Two other reasons my Alaskan experience was interesting was, one, I learned the value of denial, that is to say, there were very, very few eligible females in the area, and two, I spent sixty-three days at the base hospital during the summer and early fall of 1961, sixty-three days which, as detailed in a separate memoir, changed my life forever.

More than fifty years have passed since I enlisted in the Air Force and from time to time I think back to those four years I spent with Uncle Sam. The overwhelming feeling that fills me is one of pride that I served my country honorably for four years.

A1/C Frank Tassielli

Airplane Incident

I experienced the following memoir while I was stationed at Lockbourne AFB, outside Columbus, Ohio.

I had never felt so cold before. Even with layers of sweaters and a parka, its hood tied snugly over my head, my body shivered and the biting wind tore into my face, stinging it as if it were a thousand bees.

My shift was supposed to last twelve hours and the rifle slung over my shoulder was digging into my skin. As an Airman Third Class, just a few months out of basic training, my regular duty assignment was that of a personnel specialist. Accustomed as I was to working an eight to five daily work schedule in a warm, cozy office, this sudden call to arms, which was fairly routine on a SAC air base during the Cold War, nevertheless caught me by surprise.

As explained to me by the First Sergeant, I was to guard four airplanes, KC-97's, that were parked on the flight line. The KC-97 was a huge airplane, with two giant propellers attached to each massive wing. I had been instructed to encircle the four planes and not allow anyone to board them. Probably two or three hours had passed; it must have been 10 PM or so, and I felt I was going to freeze to death. I knew that I had to find shelter of some kind. However, on a flight line, especially in the dark, the wind was the only force I heard and felt. I could see tiny distant lights from the operations center and the control tower, but mostly I saw nothing but blackness. Flat concrete stretched out for what seemed like miles all around me. Where could I possibly find shelter from the howling, screeching wind?

Then I saw it: the wheel well of one of the planes seemed like a perfect resting place. As I climbed into that wheel well, my frozen body fit almost perfectly inside the center of this huge tire. I felt relief almost immediately. My plan was to simply find some degree of warmth for fifteen minutes or so, and then return to my circular march around the planes.

Well, I fell asleep, and was jarred into a sudden consciousness when a very bright light was shone on my face. As I quickly gathered myself and jumped out of my shelter the light was getting bigger and brighter. Knowing the consequences of falling asleep on duty while in Uncle Sam's service, I quickly slung my rifle onto my shoulder and stood at attention as the light came to a stop. My rifle, incidentally, contained an empty magazine, which was standard for non-combat airmen at the time. Four or five men, dressed in flight suits, approached me, as I stood there totally befuddled by this quick turn of events.

Had they seen that I had fallen asleep? What did these men, all officers and gentlemen, want from me as they quickly approached? I issued the standard, "Halt, who goes there?" which felt somewhat silly even as I said it.

"We just want to see if the plane is cocked," said one of the officers, as the four of them walked past me. Before I realized what was happening, the four men climbed into the plane. Surprised, as well as scared, I wasn't quite sure what to do. What occurred next dictated my actions. The plane's cockpit lights came on, I started hearing pinging noises, and as I started putting some distance between myself and the plane's nose, the four propellers, one by one, started turning. At that instance it also occurred to me that the last man to board that plane had first gone past each of its tires and removed the chocks.

"My God!" I thought to myself. "What is happening here?" As I stood there, by now oblivious to the cold and biting wind, the airplane started moving forward, towards me. I backed up. Then the plane made a left turn; I watched it roll away from me. A few minutes later it made still another left turn, and before I knew it, the plane was racing down the runway and lifted off into the night sky.

To an eighteen year old, the sequence of events that had just unfolded was beyond my comprehension. Somehow, though, I had to get my wits about me. I decided to start encircling the remaining planes, and continued to do so until a jeep came to relieve me a few hours later. As I boarded the jeep, rode to the supply barracks to turn in my rifle, and sign out, I came to the conclusion that I would say nothing unless asked, and if asked I would answer honestly and completely. I dreaded the possible consequences of what had occurred.

Well, the conclusion to this tale is that nothing happened. The jeep driver, the sergeant who took my rifle, and the airman who told me where to sign the sign-off sheet said absolutely nothing, as did I. The year this incident took place was 1959, and all these years later, I wonder what exactly did happen out on that flight line.

The Killing

The adventure related in this memoir occurred during my Alaskan assignment.

"Just aim the gun between his eyes, and pull the trigger," he said, as he handed me the .357 Magnum. He made it sound so simple, but Norman was raised in the back-woods of Louisiana and had killed all kinds of animals. Don, the third member of our hunting party, was also raised with guns and hunting in North Carolina. These guys were obviously familiar with weapons. I, on the other hand, brought up on the sidewalks of Manhattan, had only fired a weapon once before, and that was an M-15 rifle fifteen months earlier as part of my basic training. My target then had been a colorful, inanimate, straw target fifty yards from me, not a 475 pound wounded, paralyzed Caribou lying just a couple of feet from me. Don and Norm were now waiting for me to fire the weapon.

The three of us were miles from Anchorage in the cold and snowy wilderness that was Alaska in 1960, and the beautiful, but severely wounded creature that now lay before us had, only minutes before, been among several dozen in a herd. They had been galloping on the other side of a frozen lake that we had come upon just a few yards from where we had parked our station wagon.

Both Norm and Don had assumed a kneeling position and fired their super scope rifles across the frozen lake at the herd, which were probably two or three hundred yards from us. The three of us then walked across the ice and as we approached our prey we could see that one of the shots had struck the animal in its hind quarters and effectively paralyzed its back legs. This enormous, pathetic and helpless creature simply lay there, awaiting its fate.

Firmly and steadily I held the gun that was handed to me and took aim. Just a foot or two from its head I began to squeeze the trigger..... and then hesitated.

"What was I doing? What brought me to this point and this place?"

A couple of weeks earlier, Don, Norm and I had been sitting at our desks in a warm, cozy office, enjoying our steaming cups of coffee. We were stationed at Elmendorf Air Force Base, serving our duty as honorable Air Force enlisted men. The idea of hunting for Caribou was brought up by Don and Norm, both experienced hunters. Always looking for adventure, I asked if I could accompany them on this overnight trip, and they had agreed.

We left very early on a frigid Saturday morning. After driving two or three hours through mountainous and heavily wooded terrain on winding, icy roads, we pulled off onto a snow-covered dirt road and drove another half hour or so. The area where we parked our station wagon was desolate and silent and still. Don and Norm wasted no time in getting their rifles loaded; they started walking toward the frozen lake that lay on the other side of a small knoll. As we crested the low rise we saw the herd of Caribou on the far side of the lake. We could barely make them out and were too far to hear their racing hooves. But they were unmistakable – our quarry! Don and Norm immediately assumed a kneeling position, set their sights and fired.

So there I was, with the powerful .357 Magnum cocked and ready to fire. But I couldn't do it. The idea of firing a bullet into a living animal was an act I simply couldn't bring myself to do. I uncocked the pistol and handed it back to Norm who, without a moment's hesitation pulled the trigger. The sight I witnessed was unlike any I had ever seen, and I knew at that instant that I never again wanted to participate in such a gruesome act. The animal's eyes, wide open, crossed as the bullet entered just above and between them. Small bits of grayish matter started coming out of the hole the bullet had made as the animal crumpled to the ground. This huge animal was dead within seconds.

First Don, and then Norm tried dragging the large animal by its rack (horns) down the slope, with the expectation that we could more easily slide it across the thick ice that covered the lake. But they quickly discovered that its estimated 475 pounds of dead weight was simply too much for either man to drag back to the car, where they had left their knives, gloves and ropes for the gutting that had to be done.

"Frank, you wait here with the animal while we go back and get the knives and stuff. We should be back in twenty minutes," Don said.

So there I stood, alone, cold and purposely avoiding looking at the carcass. An hour passed, and then another hour and I was beginning to worry. No, wait a second, I wasn't worried, I was terrified!

"Where are they? Why haven't they returned?" The now-frozen carcass was starting to visibly bloat. There wasn't much daylight left. Our early start ensured that we would have sunlight during our hunt. By now, though, it must have been one or two o'clock in the afternoon, and two or three hours of sunlight is the most we could expect in south central Alaska in January.

Finally, I spotted Don and Norm trekking across the lake, carrying a small bag.

"Sorry we took so long, Frank, but we actually got lost and couldn't find our way back to the car."

"Okay, Frank, why don't you make the first cut?" said Norm, a devilish smirk masking his intent, as he offered me a knife with a blade that seemed a foot long.

"Um, I don't think so," I replied.

Don then proceeded to make the first cut, which emitted an ugly hissing sound as the gasses that had built up inside since its demise escaped from its swollen abdomen.

"C'mon, Frank, seriously, we need your help here," grunted Don, as he struggled with the messy evisceration. He handed me a pair of large gloves and asked me to grab hold of its slimy, yellowish innards.

I looked away as I held the squishy insides while Don and Norm took turns finishing the job that had to be done. They knew that many excellent dinners were in their future.

This entire experience was not what I had anticipated when I agreed to join this hunting party. But the grisly affair was not quite finished.

Having drawn and quartered the carcass, the three of us lay the hind and front quarters on a blanket and dragged these remnants across the lake and to the car.

It was dark by now and we had yet to set up the tent in which we would spend the night. Headlights from the car provided the necessary light needed to accomplish this next job, as well as tying the quartered carcass and string it from a large, high tree branch. Suspending it at least fifteen feet from the ground was necessary, these seasoned hunters explained to me, to prevent hungry bears from getting it.

After a sleepless, not entirely quiet night in that tent, with strange sounds not lending themselves to a restful sleep, we awoke the next morning and drove back to our quarters at Elmendorf Air Force Base, just a couple of miles from Anchorage.

Don and Norm, who lived with their wives and children in family quarters, were gracious and generous over the next few weeks as we all shared in some very delicious dinners.

My two days in the wilds of Alaska will never be forgotten. I might add, however, that I have never gone hunting since.

The "O" Club

I was eighteen years old when I joined the US Air Force, and it was a six year obligation. The first four were to be served on active duty, and the last two as an inactive reservist. The few months between my high school graduation and my enlistment in early November were lost ones for me. Somewhere deep inside me was a strong desire to accomplish something worthwhile in my life, but the path towards that goal was nowhere to be found. I had no skills nor any desire or discipline to pursue higher education. The enticement the military offered, which was travel and adventure in foreign lands, along with my conviction that they would teach me a useful trade, made the decision to raise my right hand a very easy one.

I have written about my four year active duty service with the Air Force in a previous memoir. In this memoir, I would like to write about a particular experience I had while serving at Elmendorf AFB in Alaska. That experience covered about eight months and began a few weeks after my arrival there in September 1960.

Upon my arrival at Elmendorf, which is located just three miles from the small city of Anchorage, I knew I would be living in what I considered a wasteland for the next two years. The long nights and the cold, snowy and icy conditions of those first few weeks got me to thinking, and I came to the gradual realization that a college education was the path I would need to take in order for me to achieve a fulfilling career. Through conversations with a couple of priests on the base, as well as good friends I made while there, I decided to not waste my off-duty hours drinking and carousing, as many of my buddies did. I decided to spend my spare time working at the base Officers' Club. My duties there included washing pots and pans, mopping floors, bussing tables, and from time to time I worked as a short order cook. Because my day job was a sedentary one, and I was just twenty years old, the thought of working sixteen hour days did not seem unreasonable. Furthermore, I figured that instead of throwing my money away in my leisure time, I would save most of my regular salary (a whopping hundred dollars a month) and save all the money I made from this evening job. It wasn't long after I began my work at the "O" Club that I noticed that officers were treated so much better than enlisted personnel. What separated these officers from the rest of us was almost always a college degree. That observation further solidified my goal of one day becoming a college graduate, despite my lackluster high school grades.

As the weeks and months passed my desire to attend college grew stronger. I also knew that I would need to save as much as possible, because there was no GI Bill at the time, and my father's income was insufficient to support the college expenses I would incur upon my discharge.

The loneliness and drudgery of the routine I established for myself took its toll, however. As stated previously, I was twenty years old, had no girlfriend, no prospects for one, and the very, very few I saw (I say "saw," not met) were either married, too young, or simply did not interest me. Many a frigid night, as I walked from the "O" Club to my barracks, I would look up at the stars, and ask God to give me the strength to continue. On occasion I would even stop in at the local chapel and have a private conversation with my Maker. I was working ninety to a hundred hours a week, and almost five thousand miles from home; I was very lonely.

One night in particular, though, involved a trip to the emergency room of the base hospital. In trying to free some mop strings from the wheel of a tray holder, my two middle fingers became wedged between the wheel housing and the wheel, tearing the skin between those fingers. A very painful needle plus some stitching was followed by several nights off from my part-time job. However, once I was back to normal, my routine resumed, as did my loneliness.

Eight months after I began my demanding schedule it came to a sudden end when I developed a peri-anal abscess, which required a ten day, non-surgical, hospital stay. About a week or so after my discharge from the hospital, I developed a fever caused by this abscess and an emergency procedure was required in which the abscess was lanced. Two weeks later, while still recovering at the hospital, I developed still another abscess, same general location, and once more a lancing was required. By the end of August, after spending forty-seven days of that summer in the hospital, I was released. I had every intention of resuming my sixteen hour days when six weeks later I developed an anal fistula and that surgical procedure landed me in the hospital for another sixteen days. (See next memoir.) Upon my release I was advised by my military doctors that I could no longer perform any duties of any kind which required prolonged standing. My days at the Officers' Club were over.

I spent the next couple of months drinking beer and hanging out with good friends in my off-duty hours until one December night when I heard a song that reminded me of a girl from back home. Two days and three plane rides later I began a forty day leave (see memoir entitled "My Christmas Furlough") during which I fell in love with a co-ed from Seaford. Upon the conclusion of the furlough I returned to Alaska and served the remaining months of my four year hitch. I never returned to the Officers' Club, but the eight months I had worked there allowed me to save enough to pay for the first two years of college. Although those eight months had been difficult, ultimately I thought it had been worthwhile. The rest, as they say, is history.

My Summer Without Sun

My twenty-two plus months in Alaska included three lengthy hospitalizations:

"Ouch!! Noah, what are you doing? Are you sure you've done this before?" The pain was unbearable, and I pleaded with him to stop.

"Noah" was a guy I had just met, a young male nurse from Brooklyn, NY. His full name was Noah Rosenberg and he had introduced himself to me just a few minutes earlier. It was the middle of the night and I was still a bit woozy from the anesthetic I had received before the surgery that had been performed on me just a few hours earlier.

I was just twenty years old and the surgery from the night before left me unable to void; as the nurse on duty that night, Noah had come to my rescue. He said that I needed to void and so he would insert a catheter into me. All these terms: void, catheter, male nurses, Demerol, were foreign to me. My rear end was swathed in bandages as I lay on my belly in that hospital room at Elmendorf Air Force Base Hospital outside Anchorage, Alaska. It was late June 1961, and I was in the middle of a two year military obligation with the United States Air Force. The surgeon had recommended immediate surgery to remove the peri-anal abscess that had made me feverish.

The pain of that catheter being inserted into me was excruciating and as Noah was manipulating it, it slipped from his grasp and came out, which meant he would have to begin the procedure all over again! My embarrassment during this entire episode was not diminished one bit by the post-surgical haze in which I languished.

However, Noah was successful on his second attempt, and I was finally able to void.

That midnight adventure during the summer of 1961 was just the beginning of my derriere issues. Prior to that surgery, just a couple of weeks earlier, I had spent ten straight days at the same hospital in an unsuccessful attempt to heal the peri-anal abscess that had formed by taking two or more Sitz baths per day. After the doctors released me from the hospital I thought my problems were behind me, so to speak. But a week or so later, I experienced more discomfort, became feverish, went to the emergency room, and surgery was scheduled immediately. Ten or twelve days after that surgery my doctor discovered another peri-anal abscess; and a second surgery followed. I'll always remember the comment from my sergeant, who was visiting, me, after I described my two surgeries:

"Well, Frank, now your rear end looks just like a bowling ball!"

I saw no humor in his remark.

While recuperating from the two surgeries, the doctors deemed my condition ambulatory and so I was put to work mopping floors and delivering supplies to other sections of the hospital. The main reason I was not released sooner was that the surgical procedures simply lanced the abscesses, leaving open wounds, and requiring several Sitz baths a day. There were only showers in the barracks in which I lived.

I became familiar with a number of staff members during that summer stay in the hospital, and one of them allowed me to give shots to some of the patients. After several successful attempts at playing nurse, I became a bit cocky, and one of my "patients" paid the price. While in the process of placing the needle in the upper, outer quadrant of his rear, as I had been taught, I became distracted and missed my mark, causing the needle to bend, and inflicting some pain on the poor guy. While this poor soul was screaming for me to remove the needle, I struggled to do so and had to call the nurse who had taught me this procedure. Fortunately, he arrived quickly and removed the bent needle before any doctor could hear the young man's cries. My doctor days were finished.

Another memory I have of that summer's stay in the hospital was of my repeated and ultimately unsuccessful attempts to date two of the young female nurses I met. Friends informed me that nurses were officers, and I was an enlisted airman, and fraternization between the two was simply not done, or at best rare. I guess my youthful good looks and sparkling personality weren't enough to overcome that barrier.

By the time I was released from the hospital, after spending a total of forty-seven out of the previous fifty-nine days in the hospital, I was finally released in late August, just in time for the onset of the cold and dark fall and winter months in that far off land. Friends who visited me that summer constantly reminded me of how pleasant and warm July and August had been.

However, my hospital days were not completely finished. A few weeks later a follow-up exam revealed a fistula in my anal tract, which also had to be surgically repaired, and that procedure resulted in a sixteen day stay. Afterwards, I had to endure such endearing nicknames as "my friend Frank, the only half-assed guy I know."

I would like to conclude this little saga by writing that no further problems were encountered in that particular area of my body. Unfortunately, however, two years after my discharge, while a college student, I had one more surgical procedure for still another anal fistula, and a year after that, still another.

Since 1966, my derriere issues have been dormant and, hopefully, finally and forever, ahem, behind me, so to speak.

My Christmas Furlough

It was December 1961. I had been living in Alaska for the previous fifteen months, courtesy of Uncle Sam, and had been performing my duties as a personnel and finance specialist honorably. A young man's favorite sport, however, had been uppermost in my mind, but my pursuits were mostly fruitless because that particular species of human was especially scarce in that part of the world. Oh, there were some females living in the area, but the vast majority were either married or under sixteen. Further diminishing my prospects were the fifteen thousand other airmen stationed at Elmendorf Air Force Base and the ten thousand red-blooded American soldiers five miles away at Fort Richardson. So you see, the odds were not that good.

There was, though, a ray of hope. Peggy, a very attractive Hofstra University co-ed from Long Island, had been writing me faithfully the entire time I had been living in our 49th state, and those letters had aroused certain stirrings in me. The fact that I had recently been released from the base hospital, where I had spent more than two months undergoing three minor surgeries, increased my longings considerably.

It was ten degrees below zero outside and the sun had made a very brief daily appearance when just before my lunch break one day fortune smiled upon me. A military hop from Elmendorf to Seattle to Colorado Springs became available. There would be no cost involved, and I had more than enough furlough time accrued. I applied for and was granted permission to embark on a thirty day leave. When I arrived at Ent Air Force Base in Colorado Springs I would have to take my chances on getting a hop the rest of the way home, but at that point I would be more than half way there, and a flight to the East Coast was sure to materialize. Plus, Peggy's letters had intensified lately, and at that point I could probably have walked across the Rockies.

Fortunately, my stop-over in Colorado lasted just a couple of hours. A large propeller-driven tanker was flying non-stop to Stewart Air Force Base in Newburgh, New York and several other servicemen and I hopped aboard and off we went. We would be in New York in nine hours. Though those nine hours seemed like nine days and the constant vibration those enormous propellers emitted were bone-rattling, we finally arrived at Stewart at around midnight.

There were no buses or trains running at that time of night, and so I decided to trudge across town and onto the New York State Thruway, hopeful that my uniform would be conducive to my hitching a ride to New York City, from where I could catch the subway to Astoria. I was sure my unsuspecting parents would welcome me with open arms, and some great Italian food! The three or four other guys who de-planed with me decided they would rather wait for the first bus out of Newburgh early that morning. But not yours truly. I wanted to get home as quickly as possible. The sooner I got home, the sooner I could see Peggy. Those stirrings, you know.

Unfortunately, my Air Force winter uniform was a dark blue, my large duffel bag was the same color and in the dark of night I doubt any driver could even see me. And so after three or four hours of freezing on the shoulder of the Thruway, with truck after truck whizzing by me, I decided to walk back to the bus station in town and wait for the first bus to the Port Authority Terminal in NYC. All these years later I think about how foolish and dangerous my little venture was, but I guess when you're twenty-one years old and going home to see your girl, you become oblivious to all common sense.

When the Greyhound bus arrived in New York I decided to splurge and take a taxi to Astoria. I'll never forget the smile and open arms of my mother when she opened the door late that morning and saw her unshaven and very tired son, whom she hadn't seen in almost sixteen months.

After eating, I probably slept for the rest of that day. Upon awakening and a shower and shave, I called Peggy, and thus began a furlough that I will never forget. After seeing Peggy practically every day, I decided to ask for a ten-day extension of my furlough, which was approved. Since

I had no car and Peggy lived in Seaford, Long Island, and I in Astoria, the Long Island Rail Road became my best friend.

When my Christmas furlough ended and it was time for me to return to Alaska, Peggy drove from Seaford to my house and then drove me to Idlewild Airport, where I caught a commercial flight to Salinas, Kansas. From the air base there, I was able to catch a military hop back to Elmendorf, where I would serve the last eight months of my total of four years of devoted service to Uncle Sam. Saying goodbye to Peggy at Idlewild was difficult. She was the first serious girlfriend I had ever had, and the forty day furlough left me with memories that would last a lifetime.

Frank and Peggy, Christmas 1961

New York's Finest

It was during my Christmas 1961 furlough that I experienced an unfortunate encounter with two New York City police officers. On the morning following this incident, I was awakened by my mother.

"Frankie, where is my son? Do you know where my son is?" The frantic voice on the phone was Tony's mother, and it was about 9 AM, Saturday morning. I had been awakened from a deep sleep by my mother, telling me that Tony's mother was on the phone, wanting to know where her son was.

Tony and I had been best friends since the day he arrived in my 7th grade class, having emigrated from Germany just a few days earlier with his mother, father, and three younger sisters. Five years after their arrival in this country Tony's father had been killed in a traffic accident, leaving Tony, then seventeen, as the family bread-winner. Tony readily accepted the responsibility of caring for his grieving mother and three younger sisters. He left school and immediately began working two full-time jobs to support them. Tony was always mature and responsible.

So where was Tony on this particular morning? Of course, I knew, but should I tell his mother that he had been arrested the night before, badly beaten by the arresting police officer, and thrown in jail without being allowed the so-called obligatory phone call?

This story began at about 2 AM, late Friday night, about seven hours earlier. Tony and I, both 21 now, were returning from a double-date. We had dropped our girlfriends at their respective homes in Seaford, Long Island, and were returning to our homes in Astoria, Queens. Tony was driving and was rushing to get home, knowing he had to be at his job at

8 AM that morning, and wanting to get as much sleep as possible. He was driving; I was dozing.

My first memory of that nightmarish night was when I was jolted awake when Tony hit the brakes hard in an attempt to avoid hitting the car that had cut in front of him. Almost instantaneously, I heard another car's tires screeching. I turned around and saw a car fish-tailing behind us. It had apparently been following close behind us and was forced to hit its brakes when we suddenly hit ours.

The next sound I heard was a police siren, and it took me just a couple of seconds to realize it was coming from the car behind us, which was an unmarked police car and had been following us.

Tony panicked when he heard the siren, ran the red light at the next corner, then made a quick right down a side street, hoping to elude the pursuing police car. In an instant, however, the police had pulled up on our left, slammed on their brakes, threw open their doors, and came running at us, guns drawn, and curses spewing from their lips.

Tony was literally dragged from his car, and the police officer holstered his weapon and proceeded to punch Tony about the head and face, stopping only when my friend collapsed to the ground. At that point, the other policeman came around to my side of the car, gun in hand, and ordered me out of the car. "Uh oh," I thought, "now he's going to pummel me."

He proceeded to pull me out of the car, holstered his gun, and began asking me questions:

"What's your name? Where do you live? Let me see your driver's license."

When I showed him my driver's license, which indicated that I was living in Anchorage, Alaska at that time, he became incensed.

"What the hell is this crap? What the hell are you doing with an Alaska driver's license?"

My reply was that I was living in Alaska because I was an active duty serviceman and happened to be stationed there.

"Well, what the hell are you doing here?"

When I told him that I was on official leave, he demanded to see my leave papers, which I did not have in my possession. This further incensed him, and he continued to curse me. At this point, not only was I fully awake, but I couldn't believe what I was hearing from these uniformed police officers, never mind the sight of my friend being beaten so badly and now lying crumpled on the ground. I thought that for sure I was going to get punched in the face and I felt my knees beginning to buckle.

At that point, the officers ordered one of us in each of the two cars, and drove us to the local police station. Upon our arrival, they ordered us to remain in the car and proceeded to search the trunk of Tony's car. Once again, I heard the two officers cursing a blue streak, apparently because they expected to find something in the car's trunk other than a spare tire, a flash light and a couple of old rags. Obviously, they were looking for something else, and we never found out what it was.

When we arrived inside the precinct, it was about 3 AM and we were directed into a back room where we were ordered to empty our pockets. When I placed the small capsule that contained my contact lenses on the table, I was ordered to step away from the table and they began scrutinizing the capsule. I tried to explain what it was, but I was told, rather rudely, to keep my mouth shut. At that point, the officers had coffee brought in to them. When I asked if I could please have a cup of coffee, one of the officers took a swig of his, spit it half-way across the room, commented about its awful taste and then asked if I wanted the remains in his cup, which I politely refused.

When I looked over at Tony, sitting a few feet from me, his face was bleeding and when he asked for medical attention or, at the very least, some clean rags to clean up his face, again he was cursed and told to keep his mouth shut.

Shortly thereafter, one of these "gentlemen" left the room and returned a few minutes later and told me I was free to go home, which was just a few blocks from the precinct. I did as I was told, arrived home at about 3:30 AM, and slipped into bed, stunned at what had occurred in the past ninety minutes.

My mother awakened me a few hours later, telling me that Tony's mother was on the phone. Tony's boss had called his mother, asking why Tony had not arrived at work that morning.

The next couple of days were a blur. I was scheduled to return to my duty station in Alaska shortly after this bizarre night, and the forty-eight hundred mile journey that awaited me required several flights, some commercially scheduled, and some free hops, courtesy of the US Air Force. My journey took three days, from JFK (then Idlewild) to Kansas, to Montana, to Anchorage.

I heard nothing more from Tony or his mother until about six months later. It was now July 1962, and I was about a month shy of receiving my Honorable Discharge from active duty, having served four years with Uncle Sam. A call came from my commanding officer, who told me that a judge in New York City had contacted him, informing him of my required appearance at a non-jury trial for my friend Tony.

It took more than a week before I got home. That nine or ten days included several days to process my discharge paperwork at McChord AFB outside Seattle, a few days touring the World's Fair with Jeanne, and a couple of stops in Ohio. (See next memoir.)

Before I knew it, though, I was sitting in the witness box, answering the judge's and lawyers' questions about the events of six months before.

Of course, Tony also testified, as did his mother, who had kept the blood-stained handkerchief Tony had used to stanch the bleeding. She also kept two of Tony's teeth that had become dislodged as a result of the beating.

When it was time for the officers to testify, they denied any beating of any kind. They simply said Tony had been arrested for speeding, reckless driving, running a red light, and evading police arrest.

Tony was the last person on the witness stand. After a few questions about Tony's car, the judge surmised that he was nothing more than a hot-rodding young man fascinated with cars and speed. The judge would have none of Mrs. Fellinger's evidence and tears. He simply refused to believe that these two brave police officers, New York's "Finest," would engage in the type of brutality that was described by Tony, his mother and me.

The judge threw the book at Tony, giving him ten days in jail, six months' suspension of his driver's license, and a fine of five hundred dollars. Justice had been served. I left the court-house with his mother in tears, hailed a cab, and took her home.

Paternal Grandparents
Maria DeCicco and Francesco Tassielli

Pop and Me - US Army & US Air Force Veterans

**My father, the ice man
late 1940's**

**My sister Mary and younger
brother Frank - early 1940's**

Mary, Frank, and our mother, Angela, a year before our departure from Italy

Diane Tullo & Frank on a date - 1969

Maternal Grandfather
Vito Antonio Spano

Angela Rosa Spano &
Massimiliano Tassielli
Their Wedding Day 1-25-31

Recovering from major
abdominal surgery 1967

Present Day Dude of the Month

My daughter Sharon, 2001

Author children, Sharon and Frank, during their college days

Headin' Home!

Finally, the day had arrived! My flight left Anchorage the evening of July 6; the year was 1962. The Air Force had approved my request for an early discharge so that I could testify at Tony's trial. I would be spending a week or so in Seattle, a couple of days doing the necessary paperwork, a few days touring the World's Fair with Jeanne, Stan's girlfriend from Olympia, and a couple of stops in Ohio visiting some old friends.

Those few days went exactly as planned. It was thoroughly enjoyable, and although I didn't click with any of the girls I met, I did in fact begin a life-long friendship with Stan's future wife, Jeanne, which remains to this day. On July 13th, I received my DD Form 214, officially called "Armed Forces of the United States Report of Transfer or Discharge." Although I still had a bit more than two years of inactive reserve duty remaining of my initial six year obligation, I was in fact a "free man!" After three years, eight months and nine days of belonging to Uncle Sam, the sense of freedom truly overwhelmed me. The previous twenty-two months were especially difficult. Anchorage and its surrounding area were barren and lonely; I had arrived there on September 1st, 1960, not yet twenty years old, and the only benefit of my twenty-two months there was the friendships I forged with several young men like myself.

So now I was headin' home! My next stop was Chicago, and from there I had planned to catch a short flight to Des Moines to meet Donna, a young student nurse with whom I had corresponded while I was serving my time in Alaska. But for reasons which time has blurred, and which to this day I regret, I decided to call Donna early in the morning from Chicago to tell her I wouldn't be making the trip.

My next stop was Cleveland, and I had to make that stop because I had left an old girlfriend there while serving in Columbus two years earlier. Although I was just nineteen and Marilyn was sixteen I had been head over heels in love with her, at least until she ditched me for a younger man. But the embers still burned, and so I arrived in Cleveland, called Marilyn, and, again, for reasons which time has totally erased, did not see Marilyn. I did, however, hook up with Nanette, an old girlfriend of Stan's, and the two of us were immediately attracted to each other, and began a relationship, albeit a long distance one, that was to last for several months.

After Cleveland, I took a bus to Columbus, specifically Lockbourne AFB, which was located seventeen miles southwest of Ohio's capital city, where I would stay with a buddy from my days at that station. I was intent on re-establishing a relationship with Maxine, another sixteen year old high school junior with whom I had been madly in love. In fact, Maxine was the first girl to whom I had ever pledged deep and ever-lasting love. That relationship had been abruptly terminated when her father, a First Sergeant at the base, was reassigned to England. But now, in the summer of 1962, I was almost twenty-two years old, very mature, and hopeful of re-igniting the flame between us.

I clearly remember Maxine and me meeting in a park, where we spent a few hours. Those hours were filled with Maxine's constant refer-ence to her new college sweetheart, ironically a young man also called Frank. We pleasantly and awkwardly said our goodbyes. So much for deep and everlasting love.

My journey home was almost complete. A Greyhound bus trans-ported me about five hundred miles to midtown Manhattan, and from there I took a cab to my parents' home in Astoria, Queens. A day or two later I testified on Tony's behalf, unfortunately without the desired result. A month or so later I would begin my college career at Westchester Community College, but not before I tied up some loose ends with Peggy from Long Island, another ex-girlfriend with whom I had had a messy ending. Once that meeting ended and my days as an Air Force Personnel and Finance Specialist were completely behind me, I was ready for college and I was home!

Me and Sue and ...

Sue and I met while working together at Best & Co., an upscale department store located on Fifth Avenue and 51st Street in New York City. She was a salesgirl and I was an elevator operator. Sue was a gorgeous-looking, blue-eyed blonde. It was the summer of 1962; I was twenty-one, and Sue was nineteen. It was just a few weeks before I was to begin my college career at Westchester Community College.

Sue and I had been dating just a short time, and were getting along rather well. One evening I suggested that we go to a friend's vacant apartment after dinner. Goodnight kisses on the subway made for a somewhat cool and stultifying relationship. She readily agreed, and my friend Bob, whose apartment we were going to use, made himself scarce so Sue and I could be alone. It was going to be a good night.

When we arrived at the apartment, located on 61st Street, just off First Avenue, we engaged in some small talk. I then put on some soft music and played it real low, hoping to achieve just the right mood. Sue and I proceeded to make ourselves real comfortable on the living room sofa. Our relationship was entering a new stage, and yes, it was going to be a good night.

However, after just a few minutes had elapsed, we both heard a sound emanating from a distant room in the apartment.

"Wheeeeeessshhhh....," the sound was constant and disrupting.

"What's that," I asked Sue.

"Uh, I don't know," she replied.

Our amorous togetherness had come to an abrupt halt. We arose from the sofa, adjusted ourselves, and began our search for the constant "Wheeeeeessshhhh!"

We walked into the next room, turned on the light, and saw the kitchen, but no sign of that blasted noise. The next room, a bedroom, also yielded no clues. But the sound was noticeably louder. "WHEEEEEESSSHHHH!"

The bedroom led to a second bedroom and the back end of the apartment. I opened the door, turned on the light, and couldn't believe what I was seeing.

Grinning from ear to ear, and staring at the two of us from the near corner of the bedroom, was a reddish, furry-faced animal. It was sitting on a trapeze which was hanging from the ceiling, inside a small, fenced-in cage. The cage, which was made up of some kind of wire, a little thicker than chicken wire, ran from floor to ceiling. This monkey, or chimpanzee, or orangutan (I figured it wasn't a gorilla because of its diminutive size) was urinating in a steady high arc completely across to the other side of the room. The stream splashing against the far wall was the WHEEEEEESSSHHHH sound we had heard from three rooms away! Sue and I stood there, dumbstruck, each of us looking first at the animal, then at each other, then back at the chimp.

So there sat this little monster, very comfortably perched in a squatting position on the trapeze, and obviously very pleased with himself, judging from the shit-eating grin on his face. I guess he knew he was up to no good.

The mood was obviously changed. Sue and I looked at each other for a few more moments, then walked back to the living room, gathered our belongings from the couch and left the apartment.

The next day, I called my friend Bob.

"Bob, why didn't you tell me you had a damned monkey living in your apartment?"

"Oh, yeah, no big deal, it belongs to my roomie, Jim. I hope he didn't bother you."

"Well, I guess you noticed that he urinated all over one of the bedrooms. We didn't know what to do when we heard him do that, so we just left. Thanks for letting us use your apartment though."

"Yeah, no problem. Anytime, Frank. About my roommate's chimp and what he did, I'm sorry about that. He's done it before, and it makes quite a mess. And you should smell it afterwards. I've spoken to Jim about it, but he just loves that ape."

I was real happy that Jim was happy.

My future with Sue was short-lived; subways and my lack of cash contributed to the end of the relationship. And I never again asked my friend Bob if I could use his apartment.

WCC

It was mid-September 1962, and I was a civilian once again, feeling the freedom of choice that military life could not provide. I was prepared to enroll at Westchester Community College, which was and still is a branch of the State University of New York, popularly referred to as SUNY. The two year institution was located in Valhalla, New York, a quiet and pastoral suburb about twenty miles north of The Bronx. I had chosen to attend it because it was far enough away from my family's home in Queens so that I couldn't live there and commute, but close enough that I could go there on weekends so my mother could do my laundry, and provide other essentials. Another important factor was that WCC was willing to accept me in spite of my poor high school grades, and it was also affordable.

Because my high school grades and academic preparation were sorely lacking, I was filled with apprehension as I anticipated the beginning of my collegiate career. Math and science, which were required courses in the liberal arts curriculum, and which were, to say the least, areas of weakness for me, were part of my Fall Semester academic program. Balancing my lack of confidence, however, was my determination to succeed. Almost four years of military service enabled me to meet many different individuals from across our country, and I learned a great deal from many of them. I was convinced, sort of, that any deficiency in my academic background could be overcome by hard work and a strong desire to succeed. Nevertheless, doubts about my ability to succeed academically gnawed at me.

I had read somewhere that the most successful students tended to be those who immersed themselves not only in their studies, but also in extra-curricular activities, and so in addition to demanding of myself that I study at least two to three hours every single day, I also became active in the Student Council, the Discipline Committee, the Ring Committee, and numerous other extra-curricular activities. The maxim I had followed held true and I finished my first semester by just missing the Dean's List. By the time I completed four semesters at WCC, I was able to reach that vaunted goal on two occasions.

Besides my maturity and determination to succeed, however, I've always felt that a great deal of credit for my success should go to the faculty who extended themselves to me on many occasions. As a matter of fact, prior to my attending my thirty five-year reunion at Westchester, an occasion that coincided with the fifty year anniversary of the institution, graduates of WCC were asked to submit a one page letter recalling their experiences and feelings about the institution. One letter for each year would be selected and a fifty year commemorative book would be published with one graduate's letter from each of the fifty years. To my pleasant surprise, my letter was selected as representative of my 1964 graduating class and I have included the letter with this memoir.

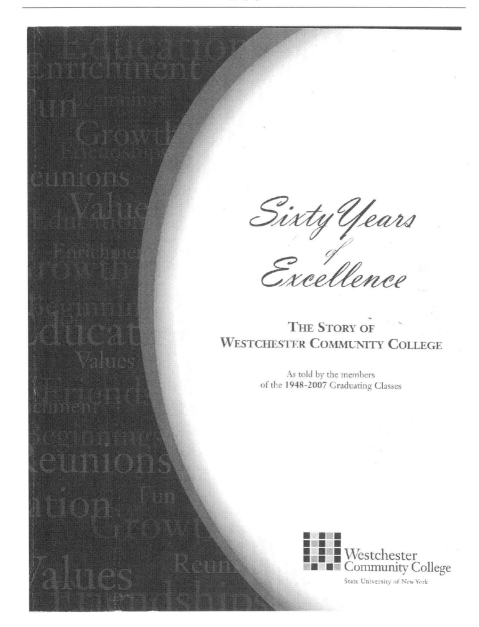

Sixty Years

of

Excellence

THE STORY OF
WESTCHESTER COMMUNITY COLLEGE

As told by the members
of the 1948-2007 Graduating Classes

Westchester
Community College
State University of New York

Frank J. Tassielli

A.A. in Liberal Arts from Westchester Community College
B.A. in English/Secondary Education from SUNY Albany
M.S. in Counseling Education from Long Island University

Frank taught high school English from 1967-1973 in Lake
Ronkonkoma, NY. He was a guidance counselor from 1973-2001, when
he retired after thirty-five years of service. He still maintains close
friendships with several WCC classmates. Frank is enjoying retirement,
spending time with his wife Diane, children Frank and Sharon, and
grandchildren Alexa and Nicholas. He enjoys traveling, reading and
walking on the campus of Stony Brook U. where he is an active member
of The Round Table, a retiree organization.

*"The efforts of all these wonderful educators bore fruit when I was awarded a full tuition
scholarship for my second year."*

Westchester Community College is now sixty years old! And it has been forty-two years since I graduated!
Hard to believe! The two years I spent there, from September 1962, to June 1964, were among the happiest
of my life. The people I met at WCC, both faculty and students, were such friendly, caring and positive
people. I remember that after having just been discharged after four years of military service with the US
Air Force, I arrived in Valhalla not really knowing what to expect and feeling very much lost. The first
person I met was Muriel Lammers of the Hotel Management Department of WCC. She actually picked me
up at the Valhalla train station and not only drove me to the campus to register for my classes but also
drove me to various college-sponsored housing in the vicinity to look for a place to live. That generosity
by Ms. Lammers was to be repeated many times over the next two years by numerous faculty members.

When my classes began that fall day in September 1962, I was rather unsure of myself and my ability to be
successful at the college level. After all, my high school transcript did not exactly inspire confidence. But
as I began to get involved with my studies and various extra-curricular activitiies, faculty members like Dr.
Marilyn Tentchoff, Dr. William McKane, Mr. Donald Mahoney, Dr. Ruth Eisenberg and Dr. Caroline
Scwelbe, to name a few, gave me their time and talents to ensure that I would be academically successful.
To these professionals and others whose names I'm sorry I can't recall, I will forever be grateful.

**The efforts of all these wonderful educators bore fruit when I was awarded a full tuition scholarship
for my second year.** After my lackluster high school experience the confidence showed in me by bestow-
ing me with such an award was uplifting, to say the least.

My experiences in dealing with faculty and students as chairman of the Ring Committee, and membership
in the Student Council, Discipline Committee and Orientation Committee were rewarded by my being
selected as winner of a prestigious Key Award at the end of my second year. I also ran for Vice-President
of the Student Council and lost by just nineteen votes. The campaign for that office and the speech I made
to the entire student body are among my treasured memories at WCC.

The two years I spent at Westchester Community College all those years ago will always be among the
best years of my life. I was fortunate to make many wonderful friends there. Although the passing years
have dimmed some of those friendships, I still remember so many of them well. Every now and then I
actually thumb through some of the now-yellowing pages of *The Valkyr*, the WCC yearbook, and see those
faces. I would love to open the next WCC *Alumnews* and find updates on how these people have spent the
past forty-two years.

Albany

Albany, the capital city, the jewel of the Empire State. Everyone I spoke with recommended it highly. Its state university, then known as The State University of New York at Albany, had an excellent academic reputation and I would love it. So said all of the professors I asked during my last months at Westchester Community College.

And so that's where I decided to pursue my Bachelor of Arts degree in Secondary Education, along with my teaching certification in English. After receiving my Associate in Arts degree in Liberal Arts from Westchester, I was headed to Albany. My two years at WCC were highly successful, in my estimation, for many reasons. But as May of 1964 came to a close, my time there receded into my rear view mirror.

In September of 1964, I arrived in Albany. My good friends from WCC, Billy and Denny, and a casual friend from there, Joe, were to be my roommates in an apartment we had found at 132 Chestnut Street. It was a three story brownstone and the four of us were to be renting the entire second floor, which ran the length of the building, from front to back. It was a spacious apartment, with four bedrooms, one and a half bathrooms, a dining room, living room, and full kitchen. Bedroom assignments were decided by drawing cards, and all seemed satisfied with their new digs. (The monthly rental, incidentally, was forty dollars per man, per month, which was quite reasonable, even then.) Billy volunteered to do the cooking, Dennis the grocery shopping, and Joe and I would clean up the kitchen every night. We agreed that Saturday mornings would be clean-up day, vacuuming, dusting, etc. The main campus buildings of the university were located about a mile or so from our apartment and one of the first decisions I made upon my arrival that fall was to sell my 1953 Ford. Living in a city not only did not lend itself to owning a car, but the expense involved made the decision an easy one. Besides, our fabulous apartment was more than conducive to attracting co-eds and my dilapidated '53 Ford didn't quite cut it as far as turning female heads.

The main purpose of our stay in Albany, however, was to study hard, get good grades, and in two years each of us would hopefully leave there with our BA or BS degree and on to better things, like a job and a steady income, or perhaps grad school. Looking back, more than forty years later, I know it's a good thing that we had our priorities in the right order because the academic program I was matriculated into was at times almost overwhelming. In those two years, I read more books, plays, essays, poems, and short stories than I ever knew existed. Chaucer, Shakespeare, e. e. cummings, Hemingway, Fitzgerald, Dickens and many more literary giants became my steady dates for those two years. Hamlet, the Prince of Denmark, for example, became my bedmate for the two months we studied that particular tragedy of Mr. Shakespeare, in that there were many nights that I fell asleep with the great English actor Paul Scofield's voice interpreting the indecisive and troubled young prince.

Somehow, our social life managed to stay alive, assisted enormously by the young distaff tenants both above and below our apartment. Having Albany Business College just around the corner didn't hurt either. We even managed to entice some of the Albany co-eds to venture away from the main campus and somehow make their way to Chestnut Street. After many trials and tribulations, four semesters came and went, and by June of 1966, Joe and Dennis received their degrees, and went on to bigger and better things. Billy met the love of his life, Gail, and although he didn't receive his degree, he seemed happier than the rest of us. However, that event in Billy's life left a void in our kitchen; in other words we needed a cook. Fortunately, a mutual friend, Mike, arranged for Dennis, myself and Mike to have dinner at a nearby apartment which was shared by four Albany co-eds with whom we had become friendly. Those four young ladies, Valerie, Katie, Faye, and Grace, fed us for the next few months for a very modest fee. At the time, they were life-savers. I needed to return for the Fall '66 semester to do my student teaching, which would conclude with my being granted my bachelor's degree and my provisional certification to teach secondary school students all about the wonders of world literature and the many intrigues of the English language, whether they wanted to learn them or not. And so, after four and one half years of living on a shoe string, which followed four years of living on an even tighter shoe-string thanks to Uncle Sam's frugality, I was finally granted my degree and began my teaching career on Long Island. I felt l was a rich man when I signed my first teaching contract, which would pay me thirty-three hundred dollars for the spring term of 1967.

132 Chestnut Street left us with memories that would last a lifetime and I'm happy to say that Denny, Billy and I, along with our wives and children, still manage to have annual reunions all these years later, even though the three of us live in three different parts of the Empire State.

Wild Ride to Cincinnati

A long, hot Fourth of July weekend was approaching. My supervisor told me that I could leave work at noon, which meant that I would have a three and a half day weekend. It was the summer of 1966 and I was working as a social worker/recreational aide in Whitehall, NY. The tiny hamlet, which advertises itself as the birthplace of the US Navy, is seventy five miles north of Albany, just east of Lake George, and less than a mile from the Vermont border.

So how would I spend the long weekend, and with whom? I was between girlfriends and I didn't feel like spending the weekend with my family, who lived in Queens. So I decided to call old friends who lived in Cincinnati, and whom I hadn't seen in four years. Stan had been my roommate during our two year tour of duty with the Air Force in Alaska, and Jeanne was his wife, whom he married shortly after his discharge. Their response to my call convinced me that the long trip from Whitehall to Cincinnati, which was about seven hundred miles, would be worth it.

At that point in my life, I had just one semester remaining at SUNY Albany before receiving my BA degree as well as my certification to teach high school English. I had little money and no car, but along with being in an adventurous mood I also had a desire to spend an enjoyable weekend seeing old friends, and so off I went on my trip to Cincinnati, confident in the generosity of strangers to carry me to my destination.

I didn't have my thumb up for more than a few minutes when my first ride pulled over. A young lady, alone, and looking for some excitement herself, drove me as far as Syracuse. On the way south on the Northway and west on the Thruway, the benefit of her charms were offered, but, not finding her especially attractive, I declined. Just outside Syracuse, I once again had very little wait before my next ride drove me to Buffalo. Fortunately, that particular leg of my trip was inconsequential, because I have absolutely no memory of it. While waiting for my next ride, just east of the toll booths in Buffalo, a middle-aged gentleman pulled up and offered me my next ride. However, he was interested in a very short ride to a local motel, where he could enjoy my youthful good looks. Albeit in a very awkward, clumsy manner, I turned him down. Thankfully, my next ride, which turned out to be with a fine young man who was quite a conversationalist, drove me all the way to Columbus. The long ride from Buffalo to Columbus was filled with some very interesting conversations, ranging from national and international politics to sports. The only unfortunate part of this free ride was that the young man dropped me off at a remote, isolated exit just outside Columbus, and it was about midnight.

So now I found myself walking along the shoulder of the Ohio Turnpike in the middle of the night, hoping that some kindly stranger would stop and offer me a ride. I probably aged a bit in the hour or so I waited for that ride, hearing all sorts of strange animal sounds coming from the trees and forest adjacent to the highway. The large trucks whizzing by were not especially thrilling either. As luck would have it, though, my next ride pulled over, and drove me into downtown Cincinnati, where he let me out at about three in the morning. That last ride was just fine, that is if you discount the fact the gentleman driving it had been drinking and the smell of alcohol and his erratic driving upset me just a little bit.

But I had made it. I was in Cincinnati. The only problem I had now was that it was about three in the morning and I didn't want to wake my friends in the middle of the night. As I looked around, aware that most of the stores in the area were already closed, I noticed a large white globe shining brightly across the street, which is where I headed.

It turned out to be a police station. I knew I had little choice as to what to do with myself in that particular time and place, and so I walked in and explained my unique situation to the desk sergeant; I asked if there were someplace where I could sleep for a few hours. Midwestern hospitality manifested itself when the good-natured officer offered me the cot in a nearby cell. I was so tired I never even heard him lock the door.

When I awakened a few hours later, I called for an officer of the law to present himself and unlock the door. A smiling policeman appeared outside my cell and asked me what it was I wanted. After my nervous explanation as to how it was that I found myself in a locked jail cell, the smile left the officer's face when he rather rudely told me he had no idea what I was talking about, and walked away.

Before panic set in the portly officer abruptly turned around and when I saw the big smile on his face, I knew I had nothing to worry about. He unlocked the door, told me to have a nice day, and showed me the way out of the police station, whereupon I went to a public phone booth, called my friends and waited for one of them to come pick me up.

I wound up spending a most enjoyable weekend with Stan, Jeanne, their young son, Paul, and Stan's parents. This young couple is among the finest people I've ever known. Today I remain good friends with their son Paul, who is in his forties now with a family of his own, and his mother Jeanne. They currently live in the Seattle area. Tragically, just four years after my weekend visit, Stan and his three year old daughter were killed in a car accident. Stan was just thirty years old, and to this day remains one of the brightest and kindest people I have ever had the privilege of calling a good friend.

I ended my weekend in Cincinnati by hitch-hiking back to Whitehall, NY. Starting just outside the Ohio Thruway toll booth in Cincinnati, where Stan had dropped me off, I was fortunate enough to make it all the way to New Paltz, NY, with just two rides, both inconsequential. However, upon being dropped off in New Paltz, which is about seventy-five miles south of Whitehall, at about midnight, it wasn't until four or five o'clock in the morning until I was picked up by several college students, who were returning to Plattsburg. I remember those hours as somewhat harrowing and more than a bit lonely. Finally, at about ten in the morning, I arrived back in Whitehall, feeling tired and very, very fortunate.

I'll always look back at that weekend and recall that experience as just one of the many memorable adventures of my youth.

1967

1967 was a year that brought changes and challenges to my life.

The year began auspiciously when I successfully completed my student teaching, and the end of January arrived with my receiving both my BA degree from the University at Albany, and a job teaching high school English in Lake Ronkonkoma, NY. My starting salary was $6,600 per year, which was pretty darn good considering that the four years I spent working toward my degree was a constant financial struggle. Loans, scholarships, and part-time jobs were the means I used to pay for both my education and my living expenses. Add to that the four prior years that I served in Uncle Sam's Air Force, which saw my top monthly salary reach an astonishing $140 per month, and so $6,600 a year was a good salary.

February was the month in which I began my teaching career. I was assigned two tenth grade Regents-level classes and two twelfth grade classes. One of the senior classes was especially challenging in that it was a class of about twenty five young men and women who spent half their school day at a BOCES site training to become carpenters, auto mechanics, electricians, plumbers, and cosmetologists. Their afternoons at the main building required that they fulfill their academic requirements.

For my particular class, English 12, Regents-level, this meant that I had to somehow keep their interest and attention with the likes of Percy Bysshe Shelley, William Shakespeare and other British literary figures. The syllabus was a state requirement, and for these future tradesmen, suffice it to say that this rookie teacher had his hands full with these non-academic-minded teenagers. Also, the fact that I was the third teacher of that school year (two others having left for different reasons) certainly did not make my job any easier.

Somehow I muddled through the rest of the semester and hopefully this novice teacher didn't screw up too many young lives.

The end of March brought the beginning of a wonderful personal relationship with a young nurse that had all the earmarks of a lifetime relationship.

April and May were filled with my learning curve in the art of teaching progressing smoothly, and a burgeoning relationship with Sharon, the young nurse.

June arrived with most of my seniors passing and receiving their diplomas, though several did so only after some deep soul-searching on my part. I spent the summer months with my girlfriend in Albany, and by the end of August several areas of my life were starting to take a turn for the worse. My amorous relationship was beginning to sour, the gentleman with whom I had shared living quarters my previous teaching semester decided to replace one roommate (me) with another (his girlfriend), leaving me temporarily homeless, and I began experiencing severe, though intermittent, abdominal pains.

September began reasonably well when I learned I was assigned to four tenth grade classes, and though I had my hands full with lesson preparations, reading, grading papers, and research for these classes I felt more comfortable than I had felt seven months earlier.

October brought a bad ending to my nine month relationship with my girlfriend, and my driving commute from my parents' home in Astoria, Queens, to Lake Ronkonkoma was sapping what energy I had.

Mid-October brought some very bad family news. With great suddenness my younger sister Grace found herself in a family way, and as was customary in those times, marriage to the young man responsible for her condition was the only option. Both my parents were visibly disappointed, and chose not to attend the wedding ceremony, which was performed in a near-empty church. My older sister Mary and I were the only family members present.

At about this same time, my one hundred mile daily commute came to an end when I found a fellow teacher who was looking for a roommate. Meanwhile, my abdominal pains were getting worse.

By late November, after several misdiagnoses, the pains were so bad that I had lost my appetite for food, and I was constantly feverish. My weight was down to 122 pounds.

I will be forever grateful to the Sachem administrator who referred me to a wonderful internist in Patchogue. Dr. Harvey Madell took immediate action by admitting me to Brookhaven Memorial Hospital, and after a full week of tests, it was determined that I had a large mass in my lower right abdomen; a day or two later a six hour operation was performed. I spent three weeks in the hospital and another three weeks recuperating at my parents' home in Astoria before I returned to my job. (An incidental, though significant comment about my two-month recovery was the fact that my mother, by herself, took the subway and the Long Island Railroad to be at my side during my lengthy stay in the hospital. Her weak English language skills were a challenge as she navigated the rails to be at my side. She stayed in my house during that time, getting rides to and from the hospital from my roommate Ralph, and some kindly neighbors, Connie and her daughter Lucille. I will be forever grateful to these people for the assistance they gave to my mother.)

It is now 2012 and as I write this memoir, I can look back over the past forty-five years and reflect on the events of 1967 with a perspective that only such time can afford.

An update:

I retired from the Sachem School District in June 2001, having spent thirty-four and one half years as an English teacher and guidance counselor.

I met a wonderful girl, Diane, and we've been married for over forty years; we have two children, Frank and Sharon, and three grandchildren, Alexa, Nicky, and Danielle.

My younger sister Grace has been happily married to Harry for more than forty-five years, and they have four children, Joseph, Kerry, Linda, and Michael, and two grandchildren, Emily and Allyson.

Aside from a few episodes such as painful adhesions, a kidney infection, a bout of pancreatitis, prostatitis and an intestinal blockage or two, I have had a relatively healthy mid-section. My ailment was ultimately diagnosed as Crohn's disease, and I wake up every morning thanking the Good Lord for His blessings.

Stan

Stan was twenty-one years old when I first met him. He was an average-sized guy, standing about 5' 6", with thick, medium length brown hair cut flat across the top, which was fairly popular at the time. He had brown eyes and a smile that welcomed all into his friendship. It was the fall of 1960 and we were barracks mates, just beginning our two year commitment for Uncle Sam in the United States Air Force. Among the fifty men housed in a wing of the large three story building, there were five or six of us that gravitated towards each other, and we spent most of our off-duty hours getting to know all about our past lives. Our off-duty hours were spent listening to music, going to the base movie theater, and perfecting the art of beer drinking at the Airman's Club. We learned everything there was to know about each other.

Stan stood out among most of the other guys for a number of reasons. First of all, he was rare among us in that he had finished three years of college, while the rest of us were high school graduates. Also, while most of us bemoaned the fates that sent us to this distant land, where the sun didn't shine for six months of the year, and never stopped shining most of the rest of the year, Stan never complained. Our base, Elmendorf Air Force Base, was just three miles from Anchorage, Alaska, and Stan saw the Alaskan assignment as an opportunity to learn about our 49th state and the sprawling town of Anchorage, as well as its spacious and mountainous surroundings. The rest of us just complained that we deserved to be assigned to an air base in Honolulu. So, while we moaned and groaned most of the time, Stan went into town most weekends exploring; he took up photography and spent countless hours of his spare time learning the trade; he developed his own photographs, too. Stan also became a skilled hunter and fisherman during his two years there. There were also many weekends that we went hiking in the distant Chugach Mountain Range.

After a few months of living in this three story concrete structure, many of us were ordered to move into another building a mile or so away. Our new housing accommodations housed two men per room and when I asked Stan if he'd be my roommate, I was pleased that he so readily agreed.

Stan and I spent about six months as roommates and we became very good friends. Although Stan was just a year older than I, he had the innocent, wide-eyed face of a fifteen year old. In terms of experience, knowledge and maturity, however, Stan was probably ten or twenty years older than I was. For example, in order to date any of the rare eligible females of the area, a car was essential, so I bought myself a used 1957 Chevy Bel Air. As soon as I paid the sergeant from whom I bought the car, he handed me the keys, and I went immediately to Stan's office to tell him of my new purchase. Stan congratulated me on my acquisition whereupon I handed him the keys to the vehicle and told him that I had no driver's license, and he'd have to teach me to drive it. Compounding the task was the fact that the Bel Air was a standard shift, but within a couple of weeks, Stan's driving lessons were brought to fruition when I passed the state driving test. On one of our first forays into the country-side outside Anchorage, as I was proudly displaying my newly acquired driving skills, my car suddenly sputtered and came to a stop. Of course, I thought the worst: I had bought a lemon; this used car was a dud and I had thrown my money down the sewer on this piece of junk. After checking under the hood for a few moments, Stan started laughing as he saw the depressed look on my face. I had run out of gas!

Another driving adventure resulted in my getting a flat tire, and there again I had absolutely no idea about how to change a tire. Again, Stan came to the rescue and taught me how to use a tire iron, a jack and change a flat tire.

On the rare occasions we would meet young girls in beautiful downtown Anchorage, Stan always seemed so much more self-assured.

Usually, the other guys and I would stutter and stumble and generally proceed to act like total idiots, while Stan wound up with the prettiest girl's phone number, and naturally, he used my car to go out on his dates.

Stan, who grew up in Cleveland, Ohio, spent his Christmas of 1961 furlough visiting relatives in Olympia, Washington. While there he met the love of his life, Jeanne, who would later become his wife and the mother of his two children.

When the time came for us to receive our discharges from the Air Force, I traveled to the processing center, which was located at McChord Air Force Base, just outside Olympia. Stan's discharge was to take place a few months later, and he generously offered to have his by then fiancée Jeanne introduce me to a few of her girlfriends during my week's stay at McChord.

The week I spent there was exhilarating. First of all, being released from active duty after almost four years, along with the anticipation of beginning my college career shortly afterwards, and leaving the hinterlands of Alaska put me in a long delayed state of euphoria.

Although Stan's fiancée introduced me to several attractive girlfriends, it was Jeanne who wound up showing me the sights of Seattle, which included the World's Fair. She was, however, Stan's girl, and there was never any question about that. After a week of processing and feeling free in the Great Northwest, I headed home to New York. My trip eastward, however, involved a stop in Cleveland, Stan's home town. Stan's generosity knew no bounds. He had had a steady girl in Cleveland before enlisting in the Air Force and although his relationship with this girl had ended, he urged me to make a stop-over in that city by the lake and introduce myself to Nanette, which I did. As it turned out, Nan was a gorgeous brunette and we hit it off right away. After a few days in Cleveland, I traveled to Columbus to visit Maxine, a former girlfriend (see previous memoir, "Headin' Home!"), after which I flew home to New York, where a court appearance on behalf of my good friend Tony awaited me. A final word about Nanette: She visited me in New York about a month later, and though our relationship was a short one, I'll always have the fondest memories of my brief time with her.

In July of 1963, Stan and Jeanne were married in Olympia, Washington, and in the next two and a half years produced a son, Paul, and a daughter, Jadena. During the long Independence Day weekend of 1966 I hitch-hiked from Vermont to Cincinnati (see separate memoir), where Stan and his family moved after their marriage and his discharge. I spent a most enjoyable weekend with Stan, Jeanne, their children and Stan's parents and two sisters, Beth and Claudia, and when I left for my long hitch-hike back to Vermont, I left feeling that Stan and his family were my family.

In mid-July of 1970, two weeks before I was to be married, I was awakened by an early morning phone call. It was Jeanne, and I thought she was calling to tell me she and Stan would be attending my wedding; however, the tragic news she uttered over the phone was so shocking that in my sleep-like stupor, which I clearly remember to this day, I asked Jeanne to please repeat what she had said. On a family vacation in Minnesota, two weeks earlier, there had been a terrible car crash, and Stan and Jadena had been killed. There was to be a memorial service for the two of them in Cincinnati a few days before my wedding, and Jeanne wanted me to attend, which of course I did.

The three days I spent with Jeanne, her young son Paul, and Stan's parents and sisters were, aside from the funerals of my own parents, the saddest days of my life. Stan was gone, I loved him like the brother I never had; I would never see him again. He was just thirty years old.

Stan

Chaos in Astoria

It was a two story red brick house, with a full, finished basement, and its purchase was the fulfillment of a dream for my parents. After experiencing tragedies and hardships earlier in their marriage, as detailed in a previous memoir, moving into a home of their own was indeed a dream come true for them.

The house was in Astoria and we moved there in 1956. We had been living in a two bedroom apartment on the upper East Side for ten years, and although the distance between that apartment and the house in Astoria was probably less than five miles as the crow flies, to all of us, my two sisters, my parents and myself, Astoria was in another world; we now lived in the country, and I can still remember waking up the first morning hearing birds chirping outside. My parents were so proud; within a few weeks after moving in, construction on a wine cellar was begun just outside the basement steps that led up to the back yard. They also knocked down a wall and combined the kitchen and dining room into one very large combination kitchen, dining and family room. Since neither of my parents drove a car, the one car garage was converted into a TV room, with a brand new TV. It was just the second TV we had ever owned.

I had just begun my junior year in high school, and my daily commute time to and from school on New York's subways almost doubled. Leaving all my friends and all my familiar places in my East Side neighborhood was difficult enough at the time, but at least I didn't change schools. I made a few new friends in my new neighborhood, but my heart remained on East 83d Street.

However, something about the move confused me a little, and actually it wasn't until years later that I became aware that I was confused. The basement, with the very large room containing the kitchen and dining area and the newly converted garage that was now a den, also included a full bathroom. The first floor, above the basement, had a large living room, complete with plastic covered sofas that was rarely used. The first floor also had a half bathroom, and two bedrooms. The second or "top" floor, which consisted of one bedroom, a small kitchen, a decent-sized living room and a full bathroom, was rented by a middle-aged married couple. What I never fully understood was why my parents bought a house with just two bedrooms. My older sister, Mary, was twenty-two, my younger sister, Grace, was just eight, so they shared one of the bedrooms. The other, of course, was for my parents. But didn't they realize that a sixteen year old boy needed his own room? Their reasoning, as I learned over time, was that I would do just fine sleeping on the pull-out convertible sofa that was in the living room. But was I fine? Not really, and I didn't complain; in fact a little over a year later Mary got married, and I moved into the second bedroom with my then nine year old sister, and less than a year after that I enlisted in the air force and left home, for all intents and purposes, for good.

And that's when the chaos began. I left home to begin my four year hitch in November of 1958. Five months later, my twenty-one year old cousin came from Italy and moved in with us. Her father was living in Venezuela, trying desperately to emigrate to the US, her mother and two brothers were still in Italy trying to do the same. (A separate memoir details my extended families' struggles to emigrate to America.) About two years after my cousin Rosella moved in with my parents and younger sister, my older sister, her husband, and their three young pre-school children moved into the apartment on the second floor. (The tenants were asked to leave.) During my four years in the military I averaged about one visit home per year, so my occasional visits weren't really a problem. But three young children, a young husband and wife living in a one bedroom apartment did present its challenges, I would imagine. Less than two years later, along came twin girls. So now there were five very young children, a husband and a wife living in the same one bedroom apartment. So where did these youngsters sleep? You guessed it. When bedtime came, they would scamper down to Grandma and Grandpa's living quarters and somehow found a place to sleep. And so, for the next ten years, my sister, her husband and their five young children essentially lived in a one bedroom apartment! Amazing! But as I already said, when bedtime came, most of the kids somehow made their way downstairs and found a place to sleep in the rest of the house.

The problem, and subsequent chaos, insofar as I was concerned, occurred when my four year military service ended and I came home to live. It didn't take me too long to size up the situation. I was about to begin my college education at a community college in Westchester County, which was about forty miles away and I briefly considered commuting. However, if there was one thing I had learned during my four years with Uncle Sam it was that I would need a quiet place to eat, sleep and study while attending college, and so I found such a place just half a mile from the college. When I did go home to Astoria on weekends, which was almost every weekend, I soon realized that I couldn't bring any books home for two reasons: first, the pandemonium created by five children under the age of five did not lend itself to study, and second, leaving textbooks and notebooks within reach of pre-school children was an invitation for them to get out their crayons and use same for their coloring and scribbling books. Also, dinner time presented unique challenges as well.

During my junior and senior years in college, which by now was in Albany, and weekend visits to Astoria were few and far between, my cousin married and moved out. Her father, mother and brothers, along with our grandfather, were finally able to emigrate to America and their family was reunited.

I graduated from college the following year, began teaching in Lake Ronkonkoma, found a roommate to share a house with, moved all my books in with me, and finally had my own bedroom. After ten years of living in that one bedroom apartment in Astoria, my sister, her husband, and their six children (another came along in 1968) moved into a large house in Suffolk County; it had five bedrooms.

A Crash and A Clash

There are two anecdotes from my life, totally unrelated to each other, that I would like to share. The first occurred in 1957 and the second in 1972:

First, a Crash:

I was sixteen years old and my family and I had just moved to Astoria, Queens. Many weekends during my first summer in Queens, I travelled with some friends to Randall's Island, which lies in the northern part of the East River, just beneath the Triboro Bridge. Several of us walked along the pedestrian walk of the bridge or rode our bicycles to our destination, which was where we went to play baseball, and to hopefully meet girls…mostly the latter.

Halfway across the bridge, one of my friends, Tony, convinced me to ride his new bicycle. Tony had just bought an English Racer-style bicycle, with up-turned handle bars and hand brakes which induced a riding style requiring that the rider lean far forward, his back almost parallel with the ground. My only experience with a bicycle had been with the Schwinn-type bikes, with wider tires, foot brakes and the rider pedaling while in an up-right position, or perpendicular to the ground.

Although nervous about accepting his offer, I nonetheless climbed onto this thing and started pedaling. Unfortunately, my anxiety was exacerbated by the fact that I was riding downhill, and picking up speed. Realizing I was going uncomfortably fast, I tried slowing down. I stopped pedaling and pressed my feet downward, as one would do with foot brakes. Oops. Almost immediately, I realized I needed to use my hand brakes to slow down, squeezed both hands unevenly, and just as immediately my front wheel started wobbling. Within seconds I knew

I was in trouble. I wasn't slowing down and I wasn't going straight; the front wheel crashed into the side of the pedestrian walk and my body followed a split second later. The side of the wall was only about four feet high, and the upper part of my body smashed against the top of it, while my lower body took the full force of the blow. The concrete wall had a rough and sharp and bumpy surface, tearing my shirt and pants.

I didn't lose consciousness but I was stunned. As I picked myself up, my friends came to my aid and I realized I had not only destroyed Tony's bike, but had almost killed myself by going over the side, and into the East River. Bleeding from all the scrapes and cuts my body was subjected to, an ambulance was called by a passerby, and I was transported to Lincoln Hospital in the Bronx. Although my injuries were all superficial, the emergency room staff swathed almost my entire back and side and part of my face in bandages. I'm sure I looked worse than I felt.

I don't remember how I got back home to Astoria, but I do remember my mother screaming when she saw what I looked like as I entered our house. I also don't remember whether or not I paid Tony for the damage I did to his new English Racer, but I do remember that we didn't play baseball that day and, more importantly, we didn't meet any girls.

Second, a Clash:

The aroma of all that seafood wafting from the kitchen was unmistakable as its pungency wended its way into our nostrils. The anticipation of the delicious-tasting baked clams, followed by the shrimp cocktails dipped into the sharp sauce heavily flavored with horse radish and squeezed lemon, the smoked eel, Alaskan King Crab legs and broiled lobster tails were beyond description. My rapidly filling stomach would require an ice cold beer before I could attack the remainder of the culinary delights: fried jumbo shrimp, linguini bathed in clam sauce, mussels in marinara sauce. The true purpose of this Christmas Eve celebration, the birth of Christ, was overshadowed by all these delicacies on this particular holiday celebration so many years ago.

We were a large extended Italian family and we followed all the traditions. This family gathering was larger than any previous one; there were forty-eight of us at my sister Mary and brother-in-law Vito's house. Thank God they had a huge living and dining room.

After guzzling an ice cold beer and some brief conversations with some relatives I hadn't seen in a while I was all set to resume my consumption of seafood delicacies. My wife, Diane, however, caught my eye just as I was about to take my seat at the banquet table. Motioning me to her, she asked if I wouldn't mind extending my break just a few minutes longer to change our four month old son's diaper. Diane was suffering the lingering effects of a bad cold and was still feeling a little weak.

Without giving it another thought, dutiful father that I was, I scooped up little Frankie, brought him over to a corner of the living room, away from the tables and most of the company, and proceeded to clean him, powder his little behind and fit him with a new diaper.

Little did I know, however, that my actions were being watched by my mother, who, after seeing that I had returned Frankie to his mother, gave me a disapproving look that was rather unfamiliar to me. As the only son of the six children she had borne, I had always been the apple of her eye. There was nothing I could do that my mother wouldn't beam with pride.

However, grabbing me by my arm, pushing me not so gently into a bathroom, and closing the door behind us, she proceeded to express her outrage at the action she had just witnessed:

"Frankie, how could you disgrace me and your father in front of all these relatives? Have you no pride? What got into you?"

My mother was near tears with embarrassment and anger at me. Apparently, it didn't occur to me that changing a baby's diaper (my baby's diaper!) was something that the mother, the woman, should per-form, *always*, and especially in the presence of other family members.

For a minute or two, as I listened to my mother's harangue, I thought that surely she had to be kidding. She was joking; she had to be. What had I done to evoke such emotion from her? I was truly clueless and incredulous.

When I tried to respond in a bewildered and protesting manner, she shoved her hand into my chest and told me to never, ever condescend to such an act again, ever, in front of all these family members. And then she walked out of that bathroom. I was absolutely stunned. After all my mother had endured in the old country, I would never intentionally do anything to hurt or embarrass her. And yet that is exactly what I had done.

The rest of the evening, including those aforementioned culinary delights, did not taste quite so delicious. After Santa Claus made his midnight visit, handed out gifts to one and all, especially to the little ones who had been good little boys and girls throughout the year, Diane and I wrapped up our little boy and headed home.

After a sleepless night, troubled and still very much affected by my mother's outburst, I told my wife about it the next morning. She was just as incredulous as I was. After all, Diane was American born and raised.

Later that day I called my older sister Mary and described my mother's rant.

"Mary," I asked, "Could I have totally misread Mom? Was she just joking with me? She couldn't really be that upset with me for changing my son's diaper, could she?"

"Frankie, I'm afraid you just don't understand our culture, and you really should. Of course, she was upset. In the Italian culture, a man is 'The King, The Boss.' He should never be seen doing woman's work. I guess that should teach you a lesson."

Having grown up in a bi-cultural, bi-lingual home, I was always confused as to whether I was Italian or American. Well, my confusion and obvious obliviousness smacked me right between the eyes. What lesson did I learn that evening? Unfortunately, judging by some of my future interactions with my wife, and subsequent reactions by my mother and father, I was simply and for a very long time a rather confused young man!

A Return to My Roots

As previously noted, August 19, 1946 was the day my mother, my older sister, and I arrived in America. I was not quite six years old, and my sister Mary was twelve. It was also the first day I saw my father, as I was not yet born when he left Italy for America in April of 1940. About two weeks after our arrival, I began kindergarten. Aside from a couple of minor embarrassments, I have no memory of any great difficulty in transitioning to both a new language and a new culture. However, I do have distinct memories that whenever we had family gatherings, which included several aunts, uncles and cousins, because I was the youngest to arrive in America, I was considered the "American," the only one to speak perfect English. The language we spoke at home was exclusively our regional Italian dialect. However, at school and at play in the neighborhood, I was thought of as the kid whose parents dressed and spoke like foreigners, and whose home always had strange aromas emanating from the kitchen. The funny looking lunches that I brought to school and the "strange" language my family spoke resulted in my being known as "the Italian kid" in the neighborhood. This dichotomy left me a little confused. Was I Italian or was I American?

As the years passed and I grew into adulthood I developed a longing to return to my hometown in Southeastern Italy. Sannicandro was a small village of about eight thousand people, located just six miles southwest of Bari, a port city of more than a half million, situated on the edge of the Adriatic Sea.

After my graduation from Cardinal Hayes High School, I joined the United States Air Force, and served my country for almost four years. I had hoped that one of my assignments would be in Europe, which would place me in close proximity to Italy, where a short flight to Bari would allow me to return to my roots and discover more about myself and my family. The stars were not so aligned, however, and my Air Force assignments took me from Queens to Texas to Ohio and finally to Alaska, but not to Europe.

If anything, my yearning to return to my roots only intensified. After my discharge I went to college and received my bachelor's degree, along with my teaching certification. During my college years, finances, coupled with the need for full time work during my summer breaks obviated any possibility of travel to Italy.

Upon the completion of my first year of teaching, my roommate at the time was planning a tour of Europe and asked if I wanted to join him. It was to be a formal group tour and would encompass nine countries in twelve days. I saw this as an opportunity to return to Sannicandro. Halfway through the tour, our group was to spend about three days touring Rome, Capri and the ruins of Pompeii. From there they would fly to Switzerland for a day or two, and then on to Spain and Portugal for the final leg of their journey. Bari was just a forty minute flight from Rome and so I left the tour and went home again. I would rejoin the group somewhere in either Spain or Portugal.

My cousins Tony and Rose and their three young sons met me at the airport in a rented car and thus began my four day trip to another time and place. They lived in a two-story attached white stucco house, which was heated in the winter by the fireplace in their main dining room. This fireplace also served as their stove. Their two bedrooms were on the second floor, and the room adjoining the main dining room was used to house their cart, donkey, goat, and dog. They had only cold running water, and a bathroom that was built about a thousand years earlier, or so it seemed. Of course, there was no telephone. The year was 1968.

I spent four days with my cousins and some of the experiences I had there left me feeling as if I had truly gone back in time. One of the customs that I believe still exists to this day is that every afternoon, after lunch, the entire family removes their clothes, puts on their pajamas, and takes a three or four hour nap. Another is that every evening, before dinner, which is served as late as nine or ten o'clock at night, the men go into the village and congregate in the town square. Some play cards, some discuss the politics of the day, and some their family affairs. The women usually stay at home doing housework and preparing the evening meal. Sunday evenings is special in that the women join the men in the town square and parade up and down the main street, with the young, unmarried girls eyeing the young, single men of the town. Following behind all the young girls are the mothers and grandmothers, ensuring that the ogling stays within acceptable limits.

Another aspect of my return to Sannicandro that amazed me was all the townspeople who had been friends with my mother and father. Many of them approached me during my short stay to reminisce about the old days, and to share long-forgotten stories about my family. Those times evoked emotions in me that left me unable to speak, especially when neighbors and friends recounted those difficult days from 1940-1943 when my mother, without the support of my father or her own mother, who had died many years earlier, suffered the loss of three of her four daughters due to a lack of proper medical care. Those were dark, dark days throughout all of Europe.

Probably the most emotional moments for me occurred when the occupants of the apartment I had lived in with my mother and sisters allowed my cousins and me to go inside. When I saw the room where my sisters died and where their bodies had lain in the hours prior to their burial, I felt that lump in my throat that left me at an utter loss for words. The same heart-wrenching knot in my throat returned when we visited the town cemetery where their remains, as well as those of three of my grandparents, were reposing.

My four days in my hometown finally came to an end and my cousins drove me to the local airport for my flight to Rome, where I would make my connection to Spain. There I would rejoin my tour group for the final few days of my European vacation.

I have returned to Sannicandro several times since 1968; the most memorable of those subsequent visits occurred in August of 1980, when my father and I spent three weeks there. It was absolutely stunning to me when I saw my father renew acquaintances with friends he hadn't seen in forty years. My father was seventy-one years old, but reuniting with his old friends brought him back to when he was in his twenties!

It wasn't until I was in my forties that I think I fully understood the confusion about my identity; I finally accepted the simple fact that I was a product of two different and distinct cultures and nationalities: I was in fact both an Italian and an American.

Hormones in New Paltz

It was the spring of 1969 and I was in my third year of teaching high school English at Sachem High School in Lake Ronkonkoma, New York. Besides my teaching responsibilities I was also the faculty advisor to the Future Teachers of America. Familiarizing high school students with the teaching profession was the mission of this extracurricular club, and we strove to accomplish this goal by having its members observe classes in session at all of the district's schools, from elementary to middle school to high school. Students also assisted teachers with many of the mundane duties that a typical teacher has to perform. In some cases, the youngsters were permitted to teach a supervised lesson as yet another means of learning all they could about a profession to which they might want to dedicate their professional lives. We usually culminated our year's activities by taking an overnight field trip to an upstate SUNY college that offered teacher certification programs. I was responsible for the planning and coordination of all of the above. Financing these activities was accomplished through the sale of candies and other seasonal items.

My involvement in the FTA, which varied in membership from 25 to upwards of 75 students, proved very enjoyable for me in that I was able to develop a relationship with adolescents outside the classroom setting. I was able to form friendships that in some cases have lasted to this day, some forty years later.

One particular aspect of this association, however, was somewhat delicate in that the vast majority of the young people who participated in the FTA were female students and I was a single male, twenty eight years old.

The experience that I am writing about occurred during a field trip to State University College at New Paltz during the early spring of 1969. There were approximately forty students on this trip, with another male teacher, Phil, a female teacher, Dottie, and one of our secretaries, June, assisting me as chaperones. Thirty eight of the students were female and two were male. The plan was for us to visit the college, have a college student-led guided tour, lunch in the student cafeteria, followed by a talk from an admissions counselor. The day would come to an end with a leisurely dinner and then retire to a local motel where the students and chaperones could unwind after a long day which began at six o'clock that morning.

The remainder of our overnight trip from Lake Ronkonkoma to New Paltz, a distance of approximately 130 miles each way, was to conclude the following day after a tour of the United States Military Academy at West Point, which was right off the New York State Thruway, an easy detour on our journey home. I thought the students, especially the young ladies, would enjoy seeing all those young, outstanding male cadets at the academy. It promised to be a titillating experience for them, as well as a reward for their good behavior on the trip.

That was the plan.

Unfortunately, however, our trip took an unexpected and potentially devastating turn. The motel we were staying at was located just down the street from SUNY New Paltz. It was approximately ten pm, the female chaperones had completed their bed checks and I had checked on the two male students. All was quiet; the long day had caught up to these teenagers. Phil and I settled in for a good night's rest.

Suddenly, there was a soft knock on my door. June and Dottie entered our room, informing Phil and me that they saw three young men enter one of our girls' room. They were certain about what they had seen. The obvious course of action was for me, the leader of this expedition, accompanied by a female chaperone, to go to this room and knock on the door, which I did. When they heard my voice, I could hear some nervous giggling and then, after a rather long two or three minute's delay, the door opened and I was asked, rather innocently, what was it that I wanted.

"Where are the boys?" I demanded.

"Boys, what boys, Mr. T.?" they responded in their most innocent voices.

We checked under the beds, and then in the closet. No boys. We noticed that one of the four girls (there were four to a room) was not present and inquired as to her whereabouts.

"Oh, she's in the bathroom, Mr. T., taking a shower."

Dottie knocked on the closed bathroom door, and asked Leslie to please come out.

I heard the shower running in the bathroom, and then it stopped.

"OK, Mr. T., I'll be right out, just give me a minute, please." So innocent!

When the bathroom door was finally opened, there stood Leslie, bathrobe on, towel wrapped around her wet, freshly washed hair.

"What's up, Mr. T.?" Again, oh so innocently.

"Where are the boys, Leslie?"

"Boys? What are you talking about, Mr. T.?"

Asking Leslie to please step out of the bathroom, I entered, noticed that the shower curtain was closed, and pulled it open. Not surprisingly, but much to my chagrin, there, crouched in the bathtub, were three strange, young men looking up at me.

"Now what?" I thought to myself. I could call the police or I could simply ask the young men to leave immediately. I chose the latter.

As the three stepped out of the bathroom and were leaving the motel room, two of them turned toward me and started giving me some back-talk, as if I was the guilty party, and seeming reluctant to leave the room.

Before I could respond, Phil, who had stationed himself just inside the door of the room, bellowed in a voice so loud that it scared not only the girls, but also the young men, who quickly made tracks out into the night. His roar actually scared me as well.

"Get the hell out of here before I call the Goddamn cops!" he yelled.

Disappointed that such a betrayal would take place, and expressing it to the four girls, we all went back to our rooms and finally did in fact retire for the night.

The next morning I decided to announce to the group that there would be no visit to the military academy, and that our next stop would be at our high school.

I said very little to anyone on the bus ride home. Upon our arrival early Saturday afternoon, I waited until all parents had been called and picked up their children. I would have to decide whether or not to tell the principal about the previous night's adventure. One of the girls in that room, Leslie, the one in the bathroom, was Senior Class President. I had all day Sunday to ponder my decision. Or so I thought.

The next morning, at approximately seven or eight in the morning, as best I can recall, there was a knock on my door. I lived just around the corner from the school where I taught and it was fairly common knowledge among the students that I lived there, but it had never been a problem. I lived in that house with one other single male and he was away for the weekend, so I was alone.

When I opened the front door, there stood Leslie, and there stood I, in my pajamas. She pleaded with me to allow her to present her case to me.

"Here I am, in my second year of teaching, untenured, and a seventeen year old girl is asking to come into my house. What is the right thing for me to do?" I thought for a long moment. Leslie begged me. Foolishly or not, I went inside, got dressed, and let her in.

Leslie took complete responsibility for the events of Friday night in New Paltz. She was the ring leader, she admitted, initiating contact with the male college students during the guided tour and inviting them back to the room later that night when everyone, it was hoped, would be tucked in for the night. She concluded her plea by asking that I not report the event to the school principal. I told her I would give it some thought, but probably had a responsibility to do exactly that. Leslie then left.

The next morning, I informed the principal, a stern individual who struck fear into most of the students and faculty, especially the untenured ones. Later that afternoon, he called me into his office, told me he spoke to Leslie and then informed her that she would be resigning her position as class president. A call to her parents followed.

The remaining six or seven weeks of school flew by. I never saw Leslie again, and I was granted my tenure the following year.

Now the denouement, such as it is: Flash forward about twenty-five years. I am at a social gathering with some friends and colleagues and who approaches me but a forty-ish young woman.

"Hi, Mr. Tassielli, I don't know if you remember me, but my name is Leslie _____."

Did I remember her? Easily.

She proceeded to recount the events of that night so long ago. She further absolved me of any guilt or doubt as to the actions I took as a result of her subterfuge. She also confided in me that she was a successful businesswoman who lived a very happy and comfortable life as a lesbian.

My Friend, Julius Caesar

I was about two or three months into my first full year of teaching tenth grade English. Apprehension and anxiety accompanied me every school day. Was I really doing this? Me, the guy who barely passed the English Regents in high school? I couldn't believe that I was actually certified as a teacher of English. Despite my self-doubts, however, I felt that my hard work and preparation, along with my affable personality, resulted in a reasonably successful beginning to my teaching career. I had already completed lessons on the short story, a novel (<u>All Quiet on the Western Front</u>), and several writing exercises related to these units. Now, however, I wanted to challenge my students (as well as myself) with some Shakespeare. <u>Julius Caesar</u>, one of the Bard's tragedies, was part of the school district's syllabus and so I began doing some research on it. This background work included reading the play for the first time.

In my introduction to the play, I gave my students some information about the times in which Shakespeare lived, as well as the times in which Julius Caesar lived. I had to rein in some of that information, though, because I didn't want to get too bogged down in history. As the old saying goes, the play's the thing.

I also knew that Shakespeare's Elizabethan English would present a challenge to my students, and so I utilized a professional recording of the play before each reading. Some of my students actually read the play aloud in class and some of it was read at home on their own, and our class discussions were actually pretty interesting. One thing I knew was that a play was not meant to be read, it was meant to be performed, and so I came up with the bright idea of having some of my students select a scene that they would recreate in my classroom. Their choice was unanimous. They wanted to do both the assassination scene as well as Caesar's good friend Mark Antony's vengeful soliloquy, which immediately followed the murderous attack on the statesman and dictator. Some of them knew that Hollywood had produced a feature film a few years earlier. Marlon Brando, who was an established movie idol by that time, played Mark Antony, and I think that was one reason for their selection of that scene.

In preparation for this re-creation, some of my students insisted on a full-dress production, which included ketchup-stained bed sheets that would serve as togas and leafy garlands to serve as head dresses. Some of the "assassins" even volunteered to bring knives into my classroom in their efforts at realism. That offer was quickly dismissed.

After reading the play aloud in class, listening to a Broadway play's recording of it, and discussing it and interpreting some of the Elizabethan English, we then did a rehearsal, without full costume, of the scenes that the students had selected, and that went fairly well.

When the day arrived for our in-class re-creation, I was amazed at how much the students were into the whole idea. Both the participants and the non-participants were eager for "the show" to begin. As it turned out, even though most of the lines had to be read from their textbooks because they hadn't been memorized, my "kids" were marvelous. One class even introduced hilarity into the Mark Antony soliloquy when the youngster playing the dead statesman became restless as the "dead body" and kept peeking up at Antony, whose reaction was to kick the "dead body" so as to force him to be still. Naturally, the entire class witnessed this byplay and erupted in laughter; it actually was pretty funny.

When all was said and done, I felt a tremendous sigh of relief on several levels. First of all, many of my students seemed to understand, appreciate and even enjoy the play. Second, neither the administration nor any parent mentioned it to me either before or after (remember, I was non-tenured at the time). And probably one of the most satisfying aspects of this experience, which I repeated for most of the seven years

I taught tenth grade English, was the fact that on occasional meetings I had with some of these students in later years, they always seemed to remember my teaching them about my friend, Julius Caesar. They didn't remember any of my other lessons, but they remembered Julius Caesar, and I was pretty happy about that.

Adventures in Counseling

On December 3, 1973, I was in the middle of a lesson with one of my tenth grade English classes, when I was interrupted by a knock on the door. I walked to the door, opened it, and was startled to see my principal standing there. Before I had a chance to wonder what I might have done wrong, the tall, thin, bespectacled administrator standing before me spoke the words I had been waiting many months to hear: "Well, Frank, the job is yours if you want it. Can you start first thing tomorrow morning?"

Of course I wanted the job; of course I could start first thing the next morning! I had received my Master's Degree in Counseling more than two years before that fateful day, and kept hoping I would be appointed to one of the numerous openings that occurred in the guidance department of our rapidly growing school district.

Although I had been teaching tenth and twelfth grade English for almost seven years, my life changed forever that morning; I had always known I wanted to work with students on a one-on-one basis. And for me it was a dream come true. Actually, other than playing for the New York Yankees, being a school counselor was the job I had wanted for several years.

The following day I began my career as a guidance counselor at Sachem High School, a job I would treasure until the day I retired, almost thirty years later. Leaving my classes in mid-year was a bit awkward, but the young teacher who replaced me, a recent college graduate, was more than capable of filling my shoes. I was permitted to maintain my position as advisor to the Future Teachers of America until the following June and looked forward to the next morning with excitement and anticipation.

The ensuing years, from December 3, 1973, until the day I retired, June 28, 2001, I encountered many different challenges as a counselor. Perhaps the greatest challenge was learning to straddle the fine line in dealing with parents, administrators, fellow teachers, and of course the students themselves. I'd like to think that I was successful the vast majority of the time.

I would therefore like to devote the remainder of this memoir to some of the more memorable experiences I encountered:

I first met Eddie when he began ninth grade; Eddie was a South Korean youngster who arrived in our country with his parents when he was very young. He was a conscientious, excellent student, but Eddie had a serious stuttering problem. His parents had seen many doctors and therapists over the years, but none yielded the desired results. None, that is, until near the end of his senior year when as luck would have it I had received the name of a speech therapist from one of our social workers, and passed the name along to Eddie's parents. About a month or so later, I was stunned when this young man entered my office one day and spoke to me without the slightest hint of a speech impediment. It was absolutely amazing. I had known Eddie for more than three and a half years, and couldn't believe my ears. Somehow, this therapist I had recommended found the key to unlocking the psychological and/or emotional lock embedded in Eddie's psyche. Eddie and his mother were effusive in their expressions of gratitude toward me. In fact, I had done nothing but recommend someone to this youngster. It was an experience I'll never forget.

Another adolescent I'll not soon forget was the young man, a senior, whose father, a New York City police officer, had been shot and paralyzed several years earlier. An only child, Ted and his mother struggled for close to ten years with their loved one's debilitating injury, which left him a quadriplegic. Ted's mother, a wonderful lady, had the dual task of dealing with her husband's lifeless form and her son's acting out in school. Ted transferred into our district at the beginning of his senior year, and he quickly established a reputation as a class cutter and a liar. I remember that Ted always had a smile on his face, but behind his pleasant exterior was a very confused young man. His family circumstances soon became known and all of our services were extended in an effort to steer Ted on a straight course. To no avail, however, as Ted finally quit school in the spring of his senior year when he realized he wasn't going to graduate that June. Several meetings with his mother proved fruitless and Ted simply faded into oblivion.

Then there was Pat, the young man whose high school years were without distinction. Pat made a name for himself, along with piles of money, by becoming a male model in Europe, and he visited me at least once a year for several years, regaling me with his bachelorhood hijinks that his bloated salary afforded him.

Of course, I'll never forget Kevin, another boy with a mediocre high school career. Kevin was involved in a serious auto accident shortly after graduation and was doomed to a life in a wheelchair. He wheeled himself into my office for many years to tell me of his struggles and adjustment to his life without legs. He seemed to accept his fate. I wonder what ever became of Kevin.

Then there was the sixteen year old young man whom I remember only by his nickname, "Shorty," who represented probably the most unusual situation I ever encountered. "Shorty" moved into a foster home in our district a couple of months after the start of his junior year. He and I developed a good relationship over the next several months. He enjoyed telling me of his boyhood in his native Puerto Rico, his separation from his mother, which was always vague in its details, and his bouncing around from one foster home to another throughout Suffolk County. His situation was difficult and confusing enough that I solicited the services of our social worker and psychologist, both of whom "Shorty" agreed to see more or less regularly. His foster parents were not involved in any way.

"Shorty" had been with us about three or four months when he was found in the back seat of a friend's car in our student parking lot. He was unconscious, apparently having overdosed on an illegal substance. He was rushed by ambulance to Stony Brook Hospital, accompanied by one of our assistant principals.

Later that afternoon, after "Shorty" had been revived, his stomach pumped, and finally returned to his foster home, the assistant principal called me at home to inform me of a most shocking revelation: At the hospital's emergency room, a nurse tending to "Shorty" had informed our AP that "Shorty" was in fact a female, not a male, as the administrator had described him.

"Frank, what in the world is going on?" exclaimed the administrator when she called me at home that evening.

Absolutely stunned, I contacted our psychologist, social worker, and several of "Shorty's" teachers. Although a couple of teachers said they had suspected something was not quite right about this obviously confused youngster, not a single one realized that he was in fact a she! The gym teacher noted that "Shorty" never came prepared to participate in gym, and thus sat out all activities, never venturing into a locker room, much less a shower.

Realizing that "Shorty's" problem was beyond my ability to treat her, I went to work the next morning and immediately sought out our psychologist, who obviously wanted to see her as soon as she returned to school, which she did the following day. And that next day brought still more surprises: "Shorty" presented herself at my office door, still dressed in the baggy sweatshirt, jeans and baseball cap he'd worn in all our previous meetings. I directly confronted her with the previous day's revelations and she unabashedly told me that she simply preferred presenting herself as a boy.

Before any of the school authorities were able to address the situation in any depth, "Shorty" was moved to a different foster home in a different district, never to be seen or heard from again.

Over the years, there were many occasions where students and parents expressed their gratitude for my part in the youngster's being accepted to the college of his or her choice. And then of course there were also those occasions where the parent and/or student felt that their rejection by a college lay squarely on my shoulders. Another source of frustration occurred at the beginning of every semester when many students and parents were disappointed in my refusal to adjust the child's schedule so that he or she could share a lunch period with a best friend. Of the many students who went on to have successful careers in medicine, business, law, the arts, education, or whatever, I'd like to think that I had some small part in their success.

I sometimes think of going through the many yearbooks that I've collected to see what memories certain students bring back. However, a simple calculation reminds me that I've probably interacted with more than ten thousand students in my career at Sachem High School, so I simply don't do it. But every now and then something or other jogs my memory, and I wonder, "What is Johnny Smith, who wanted to be a Supreme Court Justice, doing today, so many years later?" And I also think of Mary Jones, who was so sure that she would become our first female president? Sadly, there were simply too many students and too little time.

Fra-Sha II

I always thought that living the American Dream included owning a boat, and so I bought a nifty nineteen footer with an outboard motor. I had a beautiful wife, a handsome son, a gorgeous daughter, a great job as a school counselor, and a beautiful home. The only thing that was missing was a boat, and so I bought one. I thought I would proceed in this endeavor in an intelligent manner, and so I signed up for a Coast Guard boating course. However, understanding tidal charts, currents, moon-rises, and having some mechanical ability were all qualities most boat owners possessed and I possessed none of them. The course in which I enrolled had close to two hundred people, which didn't lend itself to much individualized instruction, and so I failed. I wanted that boat, though, and all the pleasures that came with it.

I owned my boat, which I named Fra-Sha II, after my two children, Frank and Sharon, for two years, and just about every outing became a misadventure of one kind or another. The following experience typified those misadventures:

It was a late summer day, and the three of us, Steve, Vinnie and I, trailered my boat out to the Short Beach boating ramp in Smithtown, where we gently and very adeptly slipped her into the water. The wind was whipping westward rather briskly, but my forty horsepower engine had just received a tune-up, so, ever the optimist, I paid no heed to this portentous message from above. We were going to do some fishing out on Long Island Sound and enjoy the beautiful day, and so off we went.

As we were slowly making our way toward the open and deeper water of the Sound, my boat suddenly lurched and came to a stop. It took just a few seconds for these three expert seamen to realize we had hit a sand bar. Our next step began a series of missteps that will forever remain in our memories as a misadventure with a capital "M."

Two of us, Steve and I, jumped over the side of the boat, and pushed the boat off the sand bar. Simple enough. But when Vinnie failed to re-start the engine and we discovered that the strong winds were pushing the boat farther and farther away from us, we knew we were going to be in for a long day.

In a matter of what seemed like just a few minutes, Vinnie and my boat were a mere speck on the horizon. Steve and I stood in ankle-deep water, and started shouting to some boaters as they passed us by. For reasons I'll never understand all the passing boaters waved to us, but none stopped to offer assistance. A possible reason could be that they couldn't hear our shouts because of the howling wind. Nevertheless, after a couple of hours of shouting and scratching our heads, and Vinnie and my boat still nowhere in sight, we became aware that the water was now almost to our waist and rising quickly.

Although we were fully clothed and the closest land was about two hundred yards from us, we knew we had no choice but to start swimming.

We arrived, wet and cold, on what appeared to be a barren piece of land, but at least hopeful that our higher perspective would enable us to locate my boat. No such luck. Where was Vinnie? We started walking toward the general direction of where my boat had drifted, and soon realized that our feet were no longer wet; now they were encrusted in yucky mud half-way up our shins. We weren't feeling too comfortable at that point, but somehow we made it over a small hill and on the other side we saw a beach and about a hundred feet off-shore there was Vinnie and my boat, anchored and awaiting us.

Once on the beach we were fortunate to find a park employee who offered to row us to my boat in his dinghy. That hundred feet, however, combined with the strong winds and roiling waves, seemed more like a thousand feet and it took us longer to reach the boat than any of us had anticipated. Our new-found friend also discovered, to his chagrin, that he had parked his jeep on the sand much too close to the water, and the incoming tide was already nipping at his front tires.

When we finally reached my boat, I quickly climbed the ladder Vinnie had slung onto the side of my boat and Steve followed almost immediately. Our friend the Good Samaritan was anxious to be rid of us so he could quickly row his way back to his jeep, which by now had water up to its wheel wells. However, as Steve was making his way up the ladder, his two hundred and fifty pounds had a pronounced effect on the steadiness of Fra-Sha II. The extreme weight shift caused the ladder to slip from the boat, though Steve, with one leg and one arm over its side, was able to climb aboard. I was sure the boat was going to capsize, but it didn't. Now that the three of us were back on board, we realized that my newly purchased and fast-sinking ladder had to be rescued, so Steve, without blinking an eye, dove in to save my ladder.

After a few more minutes, Steve, Vinnie, my ladder and I were safely aboard my boat. My engine, however, was unwilling to cooperate. As a final good deed, the park employee, who was able to make it back to the beach and get to his jeep before it flooded his engine, was considerate enough to call the local bay constable to come to our aid.

After two or three more hours of waiting and bobbing in the channel, the bay constable finally appeared and offered to tow us back to the boat ramp. We tossed him my rope, pulled up my anchor, and began the slow retreat to my trailer and car.

During this final segment of our less than thrilling day, we realized as we sat in my boat that although two of us were still wet and muddy and cold, our wives had made us lunch and we were hungry. So we broke out the sandwiches and the beers and sat back, looking astern and sating our hunger.

Without any warning, one final adversity occurred. The tow rope snapped, we lurched backward, and in a split second we were once again powerless, adrift and subject to the strong wind. However, the bay constable, with a bewildered look, came up to our side, gave us his rope, one meant for such situations and not the clothesline rope I had given him, and successfully brought us to the boat ramp where this entire misadventure had begun some six hours earlier.

I sold Fra-Sha II a few weeks later, and it was one of the best decisions I've ever made.

Beginning of the End

Charles Dickens had it right. On a Sunday, with our entire family gathered together, we celebrated our mother's 80th birthday. It was the best of days. Our family, having endured the trials and tribulations that every family inevitably experiences, was all there. Though Mom's mental faculties had been fading for several years, this occasion was to be the last of the ever diminishing moments of clarity and joy for her. And so we celebrated the milestone. The very next morning, it was the worst. I brought Mom to the nursing home and had her admitted. Two days, Sunday and Monday, a high and a low, the best and the worst. Mom would spend the first day of the rest of her life at that nursing home, somewhat confused, but ensnared deeply enough in the grasp of dementia that she was unaware of what was happening to her that morning. And each succeeding day, for the next thirty-nine months, would be more painful than the day before; certainly for her, but also for her family.

My mother's declining health as a result of her Alzheimer's diagnosis began when she was in her mid-seventies. Our family's mantra had been "Deny, deny, deny." This lessening of both her mental acuity and her boundless energy was pretty much ignored by all of us. My father bore the brunt of those five years from her first signs right until the day before she was admitted to the nursing home. Those five years included episodes when she would wander outside her home in Astoria. My frantic father would call me, imperious in his demand that I drive the fifty miles to their home and drive the streets of Queens looking for the lost and confused soul that was my mother. My older sister and I stopped every police car we saw, pleading for their assistance. Thankfully, the day she went missing for almost ten hours was a warm and sunny day. And thankfully, a precinct sergeant sent out an all-units bulletin notifying all patrol cars that a sun-tanned, smiling, grey haired old lady with a thick Italian accent was wandering the streets, and thankfully, after ten harrowing hours she was found, disoriented but otherwise in good health and spirits.

Upon our arrival into the large room, busy with the daily activity of a police station, with uniformed officers seemingly everywhere, and before my sister and I even saw her, we heard her cheerful cry: "There's my son!" She rushed towards me, cradling a fresh loaf of Italian bread, and hugged me, her only son, whom she probably considered a savior at that moment.

What had happened in those ten hours? Who had brought her to the police station? Where was her purse? Her condition was such that no answers would ever be found.

Another episode exploded upon us when my frightened and highly animated father called me one afternoon, fearing for his life: "Your mother is trying to kill me! Come get her quick, she's coming after me with a scissors!"

That episode ended quickly, with my father disarming my mother and somehow calming her, with no blood being shed, thankfully.

But she continued to go downhill. Speaking to each of my sisters as if they were one of her long-lost daughters from the past, constantly pacing back and forth, back and forth, wherever she was, urging whomever she was with to accompany her to nowhere in particular, accusing us of being mean to her. All of these actions broke our hearts, none more than her husband of fifty-six years.

"I'll never put your mother into a nursing home!" he swore to us on numerous occasions those first few years of my mother's illness. However, her erratic behavior, gradually and progressively declining mental faculties, wore him down. And so he finally agreed to have her admitted.

He insisted on staying, alone, in their home in Queens. He took care of himself, the house, his daily needs, in a less than satisfactory fashion. Because his three children led busy lives of their own, he would come out to Suffolk County on weekends, and spend as much time as possible at her bedside. On several occasions he was refused when he asked to be allowed to lie down beside her in her bed for an overnight stay. The medications the doctors gave her left her a confused and utterly vulnerable person, often barely conscious, and my father's heart was breaking, slowly but surely.

My mother had been in the nursing home for about eighteen months, barely a shell of her former self, and so the phone call I received telling me of my father's sudden passing was a shock to us all. Because my father's father had lived to the ripe old age of ninety-seven, and his older brother, at age eighty-nine, was still hale and hearty, the shocking news left us all in a daze. Upon receiving the sad news I immediately and tearfully drove the half mile to the nursing home to inform my mother that her husband of fifty-nine years was gone. She had no reaction, no comprehension, of my message.

My mother lived for another seventeen months after my father's passing, and her general condition worsened to the point that she was barely recognizable. My sisters and I continued to visit, but our visits became shorter and shorter in duration.

On April 21, 1992, one of the staff physicians informed me that the circulation in my mother's right leg was so poor that gangrene had set in. Her right leg, below the knee, had to be amputated.

God, why are you so confused and indecisive? What are you waiting for? Don't you feel it's time for her to leave this earth? Take her, all of her, not one piece at a time! Her personality is gone, her memory is gone, and her body is all but gone. Take her, not just a part of her. Please!

Our prayers were answered. That night, just after midnight, we received a call informing us that our mother was gone. *Thank you, God! The double amputation of her leg and our hearts was not necessary!*

We buried our mother alongside her husband a few days later. We were at peace with her passing. As one of her grandchildren, Linda, eulogized, "Grandma left us before she left us."

The beginning of the end for our mother, and our father, had begun several years earlier. The ravages of Alzheimer's disease had taken two lives, one directly, the other indirectly.

Dude of the Month

And then there's my son, the Rock Star.

The phone call came sometime after midnight; I had been asleep for an hour or so and was somewhat out of it when I picked up the receiver.

Drowsily, I answered, "Uh, hello."

On the other end came a young female with a heavily accented voice: "Halo, ees thees Frank?"

"Uh, yes…"

"Oh, I am so happy to speak with you. My name ees Hilda, and I am calling you from Sweden."

Almost completely awake by now, I realized the call was meant for my nineteen year old, budding rock star son, also named Frank. The nature of this late-night call became quite obvious.

"Metallix," an international music publication, featured a "Dude of the Month" section, which featured a future professional musician. It seems that one of my son's friends had sent a photo of young Frank, in full rock-star regalia, with shoulder-length hair, shredded jeans, and with his precious guitar slung over his shoulder, to the magazine in hopes of having the photo selected for one of its monthly features, and, indeed, it had been selected, complete with Frank's full name and address.

Now back to Hilda: Playing along, as if I were the rock star, I asked, "So what is it you want, Hilda?"

"Oh, Frank! Oh, Frank! I want you!"

Totally flustered, and seeing the puzzled and worried look on my awakened wife at my side, I figured my little charade was over, and so I proceeded to inform Hilda that her desire for my son would have to wait for another day since he wasn't home that night.

A week or so later another similar call, this time from two young females from the Philippines, was also answered by yours truly. And again, for a few seconds, I played along, as if I were the Dude these young ladies wished to contact.

The now famous photograph, famous at least within our family, resulted in quite a few phone calls from across the United States in the next few weeks. In addition, hundreds of letters from adoring "fans" arrived in the mail. My son, Frank, of course, played it cool, and guarding his privacy, as is his nature, never showed any surprise or signs of an inflated ego as a result of all the attention.

A couple of years later, Frank moved out on his own. He left the boxes of fan mail in our attic, where they remain, almost twenty years later. Meanwhile, my son the rock star is still very much attached to his guitar, and currently plays for three very different tribute bands: Billy Joel, Santana, and Led Zeppelin. His "gigs" have taken him throughout the tri-state area and even an all-expenses-paid trip to Puerto Rico, and another one to a casino in Council Bluffs, Iowa, where he and his band were indeed treated like rock stars.

At this writing Frank will turn forty in a few weeks, and though still the object of many female admirers, he has since expanded his repertoire, playing a wide variety of music. His passion for music has even expanded to the point where he arranges bookings. Though his fifteen minutes of fame brought him some short-lived attention and adulation, no financial wealth accompanied the entire experience. His passion for his guitar, however, remains as strong as ever, and has brought him more joy than any monetary figure ever could.

Dude of the Month

A Day in the City

The morning started out well enough. We were going to spend a beautiful fall day in Manhattan. Our first objective was to take a leisurely stroll through Central Park, then stop for a casual lunch at a sidewalk café on the Upper East Side. The afternoon, with the temperature promising to reach the low 70's, was to be spent taking in the sights and sounds of the South Street Seaport, ending up with an elegant and sumptuous dinner at the Brooklyn Bridge Café, which sits right on the East River, just a few yards from the base of one of New York City's most famous landmarks, the Brooklyn Bridge.

The three of us, Charlie, Leo and I, had been best buddies for more than thirty years. We all looked forward to this day: Three teachers playing hooky from school, and enjoying some of the pleasures of The Big Apple. Our conversation, as always, was sure to be lively and interesting. We knew each other so well, enjoyed each other's company so much.

Our means of transportation to the city was to be the LIRR. Because we knew Leo to be habitually and annoyingly late, Charlie and I both swore him to punctuality the previous day.

"The train leaves the Ronkonkoma station at 8:30 AM sharp, and it takes fifteen minutes to get there from Charlie's house, plus five minutes to buy our tickets at the indoor booth. So, Leo, to be on the safe side, you have to arrive at Charlie's by 8 AM, 8:05 the latest."

Leo's response was a very serious, "I will be there, guys, you can count on me."

You'd think I'd learn, after all these years, that Leo's vow to be on time meant nothing.

Well, it was 7:55 AM the next morning when I pulled into Charlie's driveway, and walked in his front door a couple of minutes before 8. Naturally, Leo hadn't arrived yet. At 8:05, knowing there was still a five minute window, I began my usual rants to Charlie: "Hey, man, if he's not here in exactly two minutes, I'm going back home and find another way to spend my day off."

At 8:09, I was walking out the door, toward my car, angry, again, at Leo's lack of consideration for others, when I heard his car tires screeching as he made a violent turn into Charlie's driveway. Charlie, right behind me, grabbed my arm, his daughter Jennifer, our driver to the train station, at his side, as we made a bee-line for her car. Knowing we still were within our time frame, but getting perilously close to missing the train, and feeling my anger growing, I nevertheless climbed into the back seat, Charlie in front, Jennifer at the wheel, and Leo racing from his car to ours. Just as he opened the car door on his side, and just as I was about to blast him, his car's security siren went off and Leo made an abrupt about-face and ran to his car to adjust and silence the system. Time was growing short, my patience shorter still.

The fifteen minute drive took only ten minutes but it was filled with sarcasm and a slight dose of venom from my lips to Leo's ear. "Why do you insist on cutting it so close? Why don't you simply leave your house ten minutes sooner? Why don't you shower, shave, and have your cup of coffee half an hour sooner than you normally would, and leave your house with a little extra time to spare?"

"What do you mean, 'Calm down,' don't you realize that if we miss the train, our day will be ruined? What is wrong with you? Don't you have any sense of time, and consideration for your friends?"

Well, we made it: Jennifer raced through the streets of Ronkonkoma at break-neck speed; we raced up the steps of the platform, entered the train and eased our way onto our seats with about three minutes to spare, no less. The three of us looked at each other, removed our jackets, and settled in for a 75 minute ride into Manhattan filled with some lively conversation. Just as important, I was calming down.

And then it happened: In those few seconds that it took us to get comfortable in our seats, suddenly, Leo rose from his seat, walked toward the open door, turned his head to ask if we wanted some coffee and donuts, and bounded down the platform steps before we even had a chance to answer. And just as suddenly, what do you think happened next? Yep, the train door closed, the train pulled away, and Charlie and I looked at each other, absolutely stunned by the developments of the last few moments.

In the six minutes it took to get to the next stop, Central Islip, Charlie and I had some important decisions to make. First, should we get off in CI, and if so, then what? Should we continue into Manhattan, just the two of us, and make the best of it? During this brief exchange, Charlie kept telling me to grab hold of Leo's jacket, which he'd left on the seat next to me. At that point, do you think I wanted anything at all to do with Leo?

Sure enough, as the train came to a halt and the doors opened in Central Islip, Charlie and I were still trying to make up our minds. In a flash, Charlie took matters into his own hands. With Leo's jacket in one hand, Charlie quickly rose and walked out the door. Stunned and hesitating just long enough to cause more havoc, I rose to follow Charlie. As I approached the doors, they quickly closed before I could pass through them. Charlie looked at me through those closed doors; I looked back at him. The train pulled away.

It was now 8:45 AM. I exited the train at the next station, Brentwood, and walked to the nearest phone booth to call my wife. By the way, I couldn't wait to leave that train, considering the looks I was getting from the rest of the passengers who had just witnessed the spectacle of three idiots on that railroad car. And picture the look of embarrassment that I wore, especially as I sat alone for the next six or seven minutes before the train pulled into Brentwood.

Fifteen minutes later my wife picked me up and drove me home. Suffice it to say that when I recounted the events of that morning she was simply speechless.

Dreams of Hollywood

As a young boy I loved going to the movies. Seeing those famous faces flickering larger than life on a giant screen in a darkened movie theatre became a world of fantasy for me as I was growing up. I dreamed of someday being a Hollywood movie star. My fame on the big screen would bring me riches and beautiful, magnificently endowed movie starlets would throw themselves at me. I would live in a beautiful mansion overlooking the Pacific Ocean and my neighbors would be Kirk Douglas, Burt Lancaster, and Jimmy Stewart. And I knew, I just knew that my dreams would come true. My youthful good looks, coupled with my insufferable vanity, would lead talent scouts begging me to sign a movie contract. As for talent, well….

I did realize that I would need experience as an actor on stage in order to be discovered, and so my first foray into the theatre occurred when I was in the fifth grade. I played a captured Japanese soldier during World War II, and my American captors sought secret information from me. I had to act as a brave and defiant soldier, which I did, with hysterical histrionics. However, I recall neither the applause nor the encouragement from any of my teachers to continue in the field, but I was undaunted. I continued to enjoy my movie-going experiences and constantly day-dreamed that I was Tony Curtis, and Janet Leigh was madly in love with me.

As a senior in high school I tried out for the character played by William Holden in "Stalag 17." I remember reading a few lines for the teacher who would direct the play, but he must have missed something because I was never called back. I did go to see the play, however, and I knew, I just knew, that my big day would come. Somewhere out there was a talent scout looking for me; he would make himself known as the scout who discovered the famous, dashing Frank Tassielli.

Just before my high school graduation I responded to a magazine ad asking that a photo and a certain sum of money be sent so that talent evaluators could assess whether or not I had the face that would somehow project favorably onto the big screen. I sent the money and a great "head shot" of myself. I waited for weeks for the letter that I knew would come. I waited, and I waited. More than fifty years later, I'm still waiting.

My Hollywood aspirations were put on hold when I enlisted in the US Air Force and dutifully served my country. However, shortly after my release from active duty, when I was still only twenty-one and still had all my hair and my good looks, I began my college career, and immediately tried out for the Fall drama production. I can't remember the name of the play or the part I tried out for, but I do remember reading some lines for the professor who would be directing the play. I don't know what went wrong, but he never called me back either.

Through the years, and in my dreams, I continued going to the movies, steadfast in my belief that somehow, some way, a talent scout from Hollywood would see me having a Coke at a local soda fountain joint and he would know, he would just know, that I was destined for Hollywood stardom, and sign me to a film contract on the spot. That, too, never happened.

My last attempt at film stardom took place just after my retirement from the teaching profession. I was sixty years old when an issue of my high school alumni news arrived in the mail. In the publication, it was noted that Martin Scorsese, who was a classmate of mine, though I never knew him, was visiting our school to make a donation. I wrote to him through this publication, asking that he give me an opportunity to appear as a walk on in one of his upcoming movies. Though my dreams of super-stardom had diminished appreciably, I nonetheless held out some hope. Sadly, no reply ever came.

So here I am, all these years later, and I never once appeared in a movie, not even as an extra. I can't imagine what went wrong. I honestly believed I had everything it took to be a movie star: Burt Lancaster's looks, John Wayne's stature, Cary Grant's voice: "Judi, Judi, Judi." Did I deceive myself all those years? I don't think so. As a matter of fact, I am Burt and Cary and "The Duke." All I have to do is close my eyes and dream, and I can hear Marilyn or Janet whispering in my ear: "Oh, Frankie, I love you so much; please, oh please, take me in your arms!" Oh, yes, I am a movie star, at least in my dreams.

A Death and an Insult

The call came as I was leaving the lobby of the hotel. I was in San Francisco and I was travelling with some friends. We were heading to the ball park to see a baseball game. My wife, Diane, was on the other end of the line, and she tearfully informed me that my friend Tony, the guy who was probably the closest to the brother I never had, had collapsed and died that morning. Tony was sixty-three years old. He was indefatigable, a tower of strength to his family and all who knew him. It took me several hours to come to grips with the reality of his passing. Tony and I had been close friends for more than fifty years. I took the first plane home to be with Tony's wife, Dolores, and his children, Karen and Steven.

The next three days were a blur. Tony's family was in shock; Dolores had lost her husband of thirty-nine years. Karen and Steven had lost their father. I spent the night before the funeral preparing for the eulogy the family had asked me to deliver.

Upon arrival at the church the next morning, the priest delivered his homily and prayers. As is often the case, it was obvious the priest did not know Tony personally. Just prior to the conclusion of the service the priest motioned me to the front of the church and up to the altar, where I had been led to believe I would deliver a fifteen minute eulogy for my friend. Not feeling comfortable speaking from the altar, I stepped down into the aisle, stopped alongside the casket, placed my hand on it, and faced Tony's family as I began my eulogy.

Ten minutes into my tribute to Tony, the priest approached me from behind and asked me to cut my comments short because of a tight schedule he had to keep. Stunned and shocked, I hurriedly concluded my remarks and took my seat alongside my wife.

After the burial, many of the mourners congregated at Tony's house. There I heard many of Tony's friends and extended family offer their apology on behalf of the rude priest. When I arrived home later that day, the intrusive priest's actions weighed heavily on my mind, and I decided to write a letter to the offending priest's superior. The contents of the letter follow:

———

Dear Monsignor C.:

On Friday, August 27th, my wife and I attended the funeral mass celebrating the life and passing of our life-long friend, Tony Fellinger.

Because of my close friendship with Tony, his family asked me to deliver the eulogy, which I was honored to do. It was my understanding that the eulogy would last approximately fifteen minutes. Unfortunately, ten or twelve minutes into my comments the priest who said the Mass, whose name I do not know, interrupted me to tell me to cut short my eulogy because he had a tight schedule. Tony's family and friends were stunned at this priest's actions. Over the years I have attended dozens, if not hundreds of funerals and have never witnessed such an action. After the burial of my friend, many people told me that they felt that the priest was rude and his actions were unforgivable.

My friend Tony lived an exemplary Christian life, devoted to his family and friends. For all he and his family have given to your parish over the past thirty-six years, I think he deserved a fifteen to twenty minute tribute without interruption.

The reason I am writing this letter is so that you, as head of St. C., will be aware of this unconscionable act and take some form of disci-

plinary measure. It seems to me that the Catholic Church has suffered enough the past few years and needs no further stain on its reputation.

Sincerely,

Frank Tassielli

I never received a reply.

Tony

This is how Tony and I first met:

It was Tony's first day in seventh grade, sometime during the middle of the school year, and when I first laid eyes on him, he had his arms crossed, with his head face down, and resting on them. I soon realized that Tony had been crying when I heard some of the bullies and nasties in the all-boys class sneering at him, taunting him: "Nazi!" and a few other unflattering comments were being yelled in Tony's direction.

Somehow, Tony rose above those idiots, proving himself more than a match with his superior intellect and awesome athleticism. Over the next several weeks and months Tony and I developed a friendship that was restricted to our school activities. It wasn't until a few months later, when he and his family moved into my neighborhood on the upper East Side of Manhattan that I was to learn more about him and his family's background.

When I sat down to write this memoir, I thought of entitling it "Superman" because, like the legendary "Man of Steel," the next fifty years taught me that the young man who suffered those taunts that day in seventh grade saw no obstacle he couldn't overcome. Also, like the iconic, blue-caped wonder, Tony came from another world, making a difficult and winding journey to America with the rest of his family, escaping a world torn apart from six years of all-out and horribly destructive war.

Escaping from Yugoslavia, shortly after the end of WWII, Tony's father Stefan and mother Maria, along with Tony and his three younger sisters, first traveled to Germany, where they were officially declared Displaced Persons. Shortly afterwards, a Catholic Charity organization arranged for their passage to America, where they were relocated to Tennessee. That arrangement called for Tony's family to work as tenant farmers, in unhealthy living quarters, which promised little if any future. Somehow, the Fellinger family made their way to New York City, where Tony's father secured a job as a building superintendent. The responsibilities included the maintenance of every facet of that building. In return, the Fellingers were given a rent-free basement apartment, which was located at East 94th Street.

This superintendency was the same position Tony's father held when they moved into my neighborhood, on East 83d Street. Tony and I became close friends from the beginning. His superior athleticism, his excellent progress in his school work, and his full-time assistance to his father's duties, earned Tony the admiration and respect of all on our block.

After I turned sixteen my family and I moved to Astoria, Queens, and I thought that would be the end of neighborhood friendships. However, six months later Tony's family purchased a home in Astoria, about a mile from my house. Tragedy struck a few months after they moved in when Tony's father was killed in an auto accident.

Tony was seventeen years old, a senior in high school. He immediately quit school and took a full-time job as a grocery delivery boy to help support his mother and three younger sisters. Six months later, I graduated high school, and went into military service. Tony continued to work at the grocery store in Manhattan. As fate would have it, he worked just steps from where my father worked as a doorman, and we maintained contact, albeit on a limited basis, for the next several years. Whenever I would come home on leave my father would give me updates on Tony's life.

When I received my military service discharge four years later, I almost immediately went away to college for the next four years. Yet somehow, Tony and I managed to see each other, often double dating. It seemed Tony always had a car and some cash, whereas I was usually broke but managed some contacts with the opposite sex.

Tony persevered and he and his family began to prosper in the next few years; they were even able to purchase an additional apartment building near their home. Meanwhile, a truly happy occasion occurred on May 16, 1965, when I was honored by being Best Man at Tony and Delores' wedding.

Shortly after that event, Tony began rising through the hierarchy of the grocery chain that employed him. He was appointed local manager, then regional manager. He also bought a home and although we lived about a hundred miles apart, we continued our friendship as our wives and children visited each other.

During those years I came to know Tony's resourcefulness and total unwillingness to accept the fact that there was any project that he couldn't accomplish. If anything in Tony's home needed to be repaired, anything at all, one of the family's cars, the boiler in his basement, no matter the size and scope of the repair required, Tony took it on, and succeeded. He actually built his own in-ground pool! On another occasion, Delores decided it was time to add central air conditioning to their home. Guess who did the research, borrowed all the necessary tools and equipment, and installed it? And when Tony and his family visited me and my family, Tony would make it his business to accommodate my mechanical disinclination by fixing anything and everything that needed fixing.

When Tony was in his late fifties, he underwent major surgery for a circulatory disorder. His doctors insisted that Tony cut back on some of his physical labors. Of course, Tony did not heed that advice. Tony's life ended when he suffered a heart attack after struggling to clear some of his neighbor's bushes on a hot and humid day in August 2004. However, he did enjoy every father's dream of seeing both his children marry and give him grandchildren, whom Tony adored.

At his funeral Tony's family honored me by asking me to deliver the eulogy for my good friend. With a heavy heart I did so and have written a separate memoir of the emotional day.

Several years have now passed since Tony's death and his wife Delores and my family have remained in contact. Tony's absence left a giant hole in the hearts of all who knew and loved him, and he is missed dearly. What a remarkable guy he was!

Tony and Me

Big Sister

For my seventy-first birthday, my "big sister," Mary, sent me a card which she signed, "Love, from your big sister." Although Mary has held that title for most of my life, the fact of the matter is that Mary was the second born daughter in my family. My mother and father's first born was named Maria Carmela and she was named for my father's mother, which is the custom in Southern Italy. As is also customary, nicknames are often given. Since "Mary" was my parents' second born child and obviously a girl, and my maternal grandmother's name was also Maria, then she too was called Maria, but with no middle name, since my mother's mother had none. At first, my oldest sister was called by the affectionate "Carmelina," which soon became "Meline," pronounced *"May-lean."*

Meline was born in 1931; Maria was born in 1934; 1936 brought Grazia into the world and she was followed two years later by Antonetta. My parents' fifth child, finally a boy, was called Francesco. I guess by now you know what my paternal grandfather's name was.

Meline died in 1944, at the age of 13, and what I know of her is what my parents, older sister Maria, and many of my older relatives have told me over the years.

For more than half my lifetime it was said by all that Meline was born severely mentally retarded. Unable to provide the full-time care that she required, and already fully occupied in the care of her three younger sisters, my parents institutionalized Meline sometime in the mid to late 1930's. Very little was said about the time she was in that facility, except that my parents removed her and brought her back home after witnessing the horrid conditions and absence of any proper care or supervision; her stay there lasted less than a month. Back home, Meline had to be tethered to my mother at all times because otherwise she would run away, which happened on more than one occasion. One of those times brought a great scare to my parents because she was lost for several hours and actually made her way out of our small town. She was found wandering aimlessly by a kindly soul who was headed for a nearby village. Fortunately, he was able to secure her onto his mule-driven wagon and delivered her to that village's church, where the nuns kept her safe until word reached my parents as to her whereabouts.

While in the small, one bedroom apartment my parents, four sisters and I lived in, Meline had to be tied to a chair to prevent her from wandering. Meline never learned to talk or walk steadily. One of the sadder aspects of her existence was the fact that she would defecate, then play with and eat her own feces.

As related in a previous memoir, my father left for America as a stowaway in 1940, a few months before I was born. World War II's intervention resulted in a six year and a half year absence before my parents were able to reunite. The more than six year interval was filled with abject poverty for my mother, my sisters and me. All six of us were sick with various ailments at one time or another. On more than one occasion, my second oldest sister, Maria, and I, came close to losing our lives. Tragically, two of my "healthier" sisters, Antonetta and Grazia, died three weeks apart in the final months of 1940, one from typhus and the other from pneumonia. My mother bore these tragedies with very little emotional support, her own mother having passed many years earlier, my father three thousand miles away, and her two older sisters tending to their own miseries with their own young families. Poverty, near starvation, chronic ailments, and inadequate medical care were constant companions for most of my small town's residents in those dark days of World War II. Most of the husbands, brothers and fathers were either serving in the Italian Army or had fled to other countries to seek employment and hopes for a better future. Australia, Canada, the United States, and Venezuela were the places where most men migrated.

When Italy surrendered in 1943, and the Nazi Army retreated northward, with the American and Allied Armies in hot pursuit up the peninsula from Sicily, conditions improved considerably for the Southern Italian people. This improvement, however, occurred after our town was mistakenly bombed by British war planes one night in June of that year. Ninety five of our residents lost their lives.

However, it wasn't too much longer after that particular tragedy before communication between my mother and father, who was by then serving on active duty in the US Army, was re-established, and allotment checks began arriving to my mother. The promise of the war's end and subsequent reuniting of my parents, older sisters Meline and Maria and me brought forth a quandary for my mother.

"What if," she wondered, "the war ends, and my husband, fresh from his US Army discharge and the American president's promise of citizenship in his possession, is allowed to secure passage for us to America and, upon our arrival, my severely retarded Meline is not allowed to enter the US? Am I to send her back to Italy by herself? What am I to do?"

Fortunately, Fate intervened, and my mother's strong faith in God was rewarded with Meline's passing in 1944. On August 19, 1946, my mother, sister Maria, and I arrived in America, reunited with my father after six and a half years, and for the next forty-six years of her life, my mother, while grieving the loss of Antonetta and Grazia, regretted not the passing of Meline, but the life her oldest daughter had led. Much of the events of the previous four paragraphs have been described, in detail, in previous episodes of this memoir.

Interestingly, when I visited Sannicandro, the small town in which I was born, in 1980, I met an elderly gentleman who was one of the town's few pharmacists and knew my mother during those trying times in the late 1930's and early 1940's; he told me that to the best of his knowledge, Meline was in fact not born mentally retarded. His recollection was that Meline appeared to be a normal infant until, at the age of eight months, she suffered from a very high fever, had convulsions, which, he deduced, led to brain damage and subsequent failure to develop normally. Sadly,

I wondered if even minimal medical intervention could have prevented the apparent brain damage that my sister suffered.

As I grow older my appreciation of life seems to intensify daily as I think of the life my sisters, Meline in particular, were denied. Carpe diem!

Baseball and Friendship

As I sat in the blistering heat at PNC Park, the Pittsburgh Pirates' home stadium, random thoughts ran through my mind. Was the game I was watching so interesting that I would subject myself to temperatures reaching the high nineties, with humidity indicators surpassing the one hundred degree mark? Wouldn't I rather be at home, sitting in my air-conditioned TV room, watching my beloved Yankees? How long did I plan to sit here, fully exposed to the ultra-violet rays of the sun, sweat dripping from under my hat, my shirt, and seemingly from every pore of my body? When would I seek shelter in a shady area of the stadium, and re-hydrate myself with a cool glass of water or iced tea?

The answers to these questions were really quite irrelevant. Because we were all ardent baseball fans, the thought of entering a major league baseball park, with its vast expanse of lush, green, meticulously groomed grass, then taking in its smell, was quite appealing. Along with the feeling was the buzz and the general excitement of being among thousands and thousands of other people with the same interest, and so the four of us had made a pact, which was to visit all of the thirty major league baseball stadiums in America. Visiting PNC Park was the twenty-third of thirty major league baseball parks we had seen. Our pact was made sometime in 1990. At that time, the four of us, Ishy, Richie, Pete and I, agreed it would be a great idea if, every summer, beginning that year, we would visit one or two major league baseball stadiums, and we would do so until we had seen them all.

So, having survived the sweltering heat of Pittsburgh this past summer, we began discussing our next trip, scheduled to take place in the spring or summer of 2012. We also reviewed some of our past experiences in this lengthy quest.

The very first stadium we saw, in August of 1990, was Fenway Park, known for its "Green Monster" in left field, as well as having the shortest distance from home plate to the right field foul pole in all of baseball. The location, of course, was Boston, Massachusetts. Our two night trip had the four of us sharing one rather tiny motel room. We had many lively conversations that weekend, and generally got along well, and so we easily decided to continue our annual jaunts.

However, for reasons that today we cannot remember, the remainder of the 1990's was somewhat inconsistent in our quest:

1991 and 1992 saw us visit Philadelphia's Veterans' Stadium, which no longer exists, having been replaced by the ultra-modern Citizens' Bank Park, and Camden Yards, home of the Baltimore Orioles, respectively. The years 1993-1997 inexplicably saw a return to Fenway Park (1996), with no trips in 1994-95 and 97. Our goal resumed, sort of, in 1998, with an early and a late summer trip to Norwich, Connecticut, home of the New York Yankees Double A team, the Norwich Navigators. The reason for the second trip to Norwich in late summer was due to the early summer's game being postponed when a violent thunderstorm struck, sending thousands of fans rushing en-masse to their cars to escape the dangerous winds that accompanied the sudden deluge.

1999 proved to be the beginning of a consistent, annual trek to achieve our ultimate goal. Cleveland's Memorial Stadium, the "mistake by the lake," with its mammoth capacity of 80,000 fans, was torn down in 1996, and replaced with beautiful Jacobs Field, with its terrific sight lines from every seat in the spacious ball park.

After 1999, we resumed our quest with annual trips across our country. We saw the famous ivy-covered outfield walls of the Chicago Cubs' Wrigley Field, the Brooklyn Dodgers' new team and adopted city of Los Angeles, with its beautifully maintained Dodger Stadium, nestled in cozy Chavez Ravine. We were treated to the wondrous sight of the Budweiser Clydesdales – truly magnificent creatures - as they gallantly trotted along the warning tracks and foul territories of Busch Stadium, home of the St. Louis Cardinals.

The last several years, with all of us having retired from the teaching profession, and passing the age of sixty, splurging on high end hotels, two to a room, became the norm. Also improving our goal was the fact that my son, Frank, and I, began visiting ball parks where our Yankees were the visiting team. In recent years, we saw the Bronx Bombers play in Atlanta, Pittsburgh, Toronto, and Philadelphia. These trips will probably not hasten the pact I made with my three pals, but they are a source of great satisfaction to me in that I get to spend quality time with my boy.

Wrigley Field in Chicago, home of the Cubs, the team with the longest tenure for not winning a World Series (1908 was the last time they won, and 1945 was the last time the Cubbies even appeared in a World Series!) was easily the favorite stadium we have visited. An added treat at Wrigley was hearing and seeing the beautiful Barbara Eden of TV's "I Dream of Jeannie," fame singing "Take Me Out to the Ball Game" during the seventh inning stretch.

The San Francisco Giants' stadium, located on the edge of San Francisco Bay, is probably the second most beautiful stadium we've visited. By contrast, Shea Stadium, home of the New York Mets, Robert F. Kennedy Stadium, home of the Washington Nationals, and County Stadium in Milwaukee, home of the Brewers, were three dilapidated and depressing ball parks, which thankfully underwent demolition the year after our visit.

Our trip to the Bay Area of San Francisco-Oakland in 2004 featured a tour of one of America's most beautiful cities. That trip was sadly cut short when I returned home a few days early due to the sudden passing of my life-long and beloved friend, Tony Fellinger.

Sad too was the year 2008 in that one of our foursome, Ishy, moved to Florida to care for his elderly parents, and was no longer able to accompany us on future trips. Fortunately for us, our good friend, Jim, was able to fill in quite nicely.

2009 saw us make our first early spring trip as we flew to Houston, Texas, and saw the beautiful and spacious home of the Houston Astros, known as Minute Maid Park. A four hour drive up to Dallas to see the Texas Rangers was over-shadowed by our guided tour of the JFK Assassination site, and Parkman Cemetery, where we viewed the final resting place of Yankee icon Mickey Mantle.

Another of the highlights of our travels occurred in 2008, when my son and I traveled to Pittsburgh, where our Yankees visited the Pirates for the first time since their 1960 World Series loss. Fate intervened in a pleasant way when we spotted the Yankee manager, Joe Girardi, sitting alone in a hotel coffee shop. As politely as we could, we asked the Yankee skipper if he would pose for a photo and sign a baseball, which he happily did. A great moment!

All these years later, as I look back on all the stadiums we've visited, there is no question that the feeling a fan gets upon walking into a ballpark, whether with my good friends, or my son, simply cannot be recreated on the evening news or the morning's sports pages. An ancillary treat to these trips is visiting some of the sights each city has to offer: Babe Ruth's museum in Baltimore, Alcatraz in San Francisco, the Rock and Roll Hall of Fame in Cleveland, the famous Arch of St. Louis, the latter fondly remembered for our discovery that one of our foursome suffered from claustrophobia, thus rendering him incapable of entering the tiny capsule that lifts tourists to the apex of the Arch. Our somber visits to the mausoleums housing the remains of famous comedian Lou Costello, and New York Yankee icon Mickey Mantle stand out, as do the grave sites of Hollywood movie star Greer Garson, and Dallas Cowboy coach Tom Landry. Meeting, greeting and having a photo taken with a New York Met player, John Franco, who was on one of our flights, similar meetings with hockey and baseball announcer Howie Rose, Yankee coach Tony Pena, Met pitcher Steve Trachsel, however brief, were nonetheless memorable in their own right. All those experiences, however, pale, in my estimation, to the camaraderie built up over the years with my dear friends Pete, the "walking encyclopedia," Ishy, the good-hearted and generous Hungarian, Richie, with his devilish sense of humor, and Jimmy, in his precise and tranquil way. These are my life-long buddies who enrich our annual trips.

If I'm Italian, Why Can't I Speak the Language?

I was almost six years old when I arrived in America and I have no memory of having to learn a new language. Throughout my childhood and into my early adulthood the language spoken in my home was exclusively Italian, or what I thought was Italian. My mother, father, and two sisters rarely, if ever, spoke English at home. My folks had a very active social life, and so we always had company in our home. The people who came over were relatives and close friends, and everyone spoke Italian. Our Italian, it was explained to me, was really a dialect spoken by residents of the many small towns in close proximity to Bari, a large city located in Southeastern Italy. Each town spoke a slightly different version of this Baresi dialect and our version was called Sannicandresi because we lived in Sannicandro. Our dialect was a conversational one, not a written one. The only people who came into our home who were not from our village were those individuals who married someone from our village. Those people were referred to as "straniero," or foreigners, behind their backs of course. I'm not accusing my parents of xenophobia, mind you; I just think they were more comfortable with their own kind.

During my high school years, my military service years, and my college years, I spoke English outside my home and "Italian" at home. Although I became aware that my dialect differed somewhat from the formal Italian language, I believed these differences were minor. I was born in Italy, I was Italian, my entire family spoke Italian, and that was that.

It wasn't until I was twenty-seven years old, when I visited my cousins in Sannicandro for a few days that the reality that I could neither speak nor understand Italian hit me square between the eyes. As noted in a separate memoir, my visit to Sannicandro occurred half-way through a formal, guided tour of a twelve day, eight country trip I was on. In the middle of the tour, I left my group in Rome and flew to Bari. This side trip would be the realization of a dream I'd had for many years. It was my first return to my birthplace, the town I had left twenty-two years earlier. It was a return to my roots.

During those few days with my cousins we left our village a couple of times to do some shopping in the big city, Bari. It was during these excursions, when I heard my cousins speak to merchants in the real Italian, that I realized the chasm that existed between what I had always thought was the Italian language and the "real" Italian.

I wondered, "How could this be? Why do I feel like a foreigner in the country of my birth?" I reflected back on previous occasions in my life when someone spoke this formal Italian, whether it was in a movie theatre, a restaurant, or at various times during my career as a teacher and guidance counselor, and I was asked to translate. I remember being embarrassed that I wasn't able to be an effective translator. I dismissed those occasions by explaining that they must be speaking in an unusual dialect, though I did in fact realize that something wasn't quite right.

However, an encounter I'd had just a few days earlier on my tour, while with my travel group in Rome, should have convinced me of this reality. Our bus driver, a Dutchman who spoke no Italian, had double-parked our bus on a busy street and a polizia was about to issue a summons.

"Hold on," our tour guide shouted at the officer.

"We have a young man here who can explain to you that we were just leaving! Frank, come quickly; explain to the officer that we were just getting ready to leave, and to please not give us the parking ticket!"

After about fifteen or twenty minutes of pleading with the policeman, his growing irritation at our failed attempt to communicate ended with his repeated exclamation, "Testa dura! Testa dura!" He handed the driver the summons and walked away, scratching his head, and muttering some obvious curse words which were pretty much universally understood!

"What happened, Frank?" my travel companions asked. I was both dumbfounded and confounded, as well as embarrassed. I learned later on that "testa dura" meant "hard headed." In my dialect, hard headed was "capa toste."

Why hadn't I been able to speak to and understand that man? And why hadn't I ever studied the formal Italian as a school boy?

The reasons:

In junior high, I had a choice between Spanish and German (no Italian was offered) and I chose German because it was rumored that gang members were in the Spanish class.

When I entered Cardinal Hayes High School I was placed in an advanced German class, even though Italian was offered at the school. The reasoning was that I had done pretty well in my previous two years of German studies. As it turned out, that was a big mistake, as indicated in a memoir about my experiences at Hayes.

Four years later, upon the conclusion of my military service, and upon my entrance to community college, Italian was not offered, and my choices were either French or German. Guess which one I chose?

Upon my transfer to Albany State University, my foreign language requirements were fulfilled and my course load was filled with my chosen major, English, secondary education, and my minor field, psychology.

By the time I began my teaching career, I was pursuing my MS degree in Counseling and there was no language requirement.

I have many first cousins who have migrated to America over the years, and every single one of them speaks both our dialect and the formal Italian. Their parents, however, as with my parents, speak a little of the formal Italian, but converse in our dialect. Here, once again, are the reasons:

All of my first cousins came to this country when they were in their late teens, twenties or thirties, and so had studied the formal Italian in their school days in Italy. All of my aunts and uncles, as well as my parents, had very little formal education and in their time dialect was "the" language. My mother, for example, left school after first grade, my father after third grade. Our grandparents had no formal education of any kind.

In my older and retired years I have made a couple of half-hearted attempts to study formal Italian. Each time, however, I found the frustration level too high, and simply reverted to my knowledge of our dialect.

Over the years, Italian-speaking people have given me very strange looks when I spoke to them in my Italian dialect.

"Are you sure you're Italian?" is a typical query. To give you some idea of the differences between my dialect and the formal Italian I have listed below a few examples:

English	Italian	Sannicandresi dialect
Father	Padre	Watown
Wine	Vino	Meer
Tomorrow	Domani	Craw
Olives	Olive	Yawoy
Girl	Ragazza	Peechewed
Boy	Ragazzo	Walyo
Tomato	Pomodoro	Maranjeed

I hope you believe me: I *am* Italian!

According to many relatives I've spoken to over the years, when Italy was first united in 1861, very few Italians actually spoke Italian. The vast majority spoke many, many regional dialects. Today, practically every Italian speaks Italian to varying degrees of fluency. This shift has come at the expense of the dialects. Although very few Italians speak dialect in the home, even fewer speak it in social settings.

Cousins

I have seventeen first cousins, (thirty-four if you count their spouses, which I do) and I am the third youngest. Four of my cousins were born in the United States; the rest (myself included) were born in Sannicandro, Bari, Italy. All thirteen of my cousins who were born in Italy had completed their education prior to their arrival here. Since I was just under six years of age when I arrived, I obviously had all my education in America. Some of my cousins arrived in their late teens, some in their twenties, some in their thirties, and the last of them, my second oldest cousin, Tony, arrived with his wife, Rosa, and three young sons, in 1970. They were in their early forties. Of my seventeen first cousins, only Rosalie, her husband Dominic, and their three children, remained in Italy, and have lived in Monopoli, a city of about fifty thousand roughly fifty miles from Sannicandro. Another of my cousins, Frank, lived and worked in New York, and when he retired he moved back to Sannicandro, where he lives with his wife, son, daughter-in-law and grandchildren.

I have always held my cousins in the highest esteem, primarily because I saw how kind, caring, loving, generous and respectful they were towards my mother and father. Another reason I grew to respect all of them is because they all adapted successfully to this country, in their chosen vocations as well as in their respective communities and all have become naturalized American citizens.

Here are some of my cousins' accomplishments:

For example, my Aunt Donata and Uncle Luigi's seven children bore them sixteen grandsons and just four granddaughters! Another of my cousins, Jerry, became a highly successful businessman, first owning his own home heating oil business, selling it and then becoming the owner of two motels. Following that, in his later years, he sold the motels and became a home builder.

Other cousins were also successful owners of a plumbing company (Joe), a carting and disposal company (Frank), a wholesale fruit delivery business (Tony and Rocky), and two became teachers and administrators (Jean and Mary). One of these educators was an elementary school teacher for fifty-five years!

When my mother, my older sister and I arrived in America, it was my cousin Gennaro (Jerry) and his wife Angela (Lina), who embraced us and smoothed our transition to a new culture and language. When my third oldest cousin, Vito, arrived in this country in the same manner as my father (illegally), it was with great pride as I observed him adjust to his new way of life, marrying, raising a family, and becoming a successful businessman; he too became a naturalized American citizen. Another of my cousins, Vitantonio, (Tony) arrived in this country in his late teens and within two years of his arrival served with the US Army in Korea during the Korean War.

When I visited Sannicandro for the first time, twenty-two years after I had left it, one of my cousins, Tony and his wife Rosa, housed me, fed me and generally took good care of me during my visit there.

On my wedding day, my second youngest cousin, Frank, honored me by serving as my Best Man.

My family has always been close knit. When my cousin Rosella arrived in America by herself as a single young woman at the age of twenty-one, she lived with my mother and father, my two sisters and myself for five years, until her own family was able to reunite here in America.

Every one of my first cousins' spouses has become my friend, and for the past five years or so, several of us have gathered together for annual visits at the Pt. Pleasant Beach, New Jersey home of Barbara and Frank. There we have feasted on shared memories, good Italian food, and lively discussions that ranged from A to Z.

On those occasions when I get together with any of my cousins, very often we exchange stories and memories from days gone by, when our parents were still with us. I am quite certain that although our parents are no longer with us, (none, that is, except for my father's youngest sibling, his sister Vincenza, who is ninety-five years young at the time of this writing) they exchange smiles in Heaven in the knowledge that their children still share strong bonds, bonds that hopefully will be carried on by future generations.

My Father, Massimiliano

My father, Massimiliano Tassielli, was born in Sannicandro, Italy, on Sept. 14, 1908, to Francesco and Maria Carmela DeCicco Tassielli. He was the youngest of three sons, and attended school until the end of second grade and, at the age of 7, joined his father and two older brothers to work the land for their sustenance. When my father turned eight, his oldest brother, Vincenzo, was drafted into the Italian Army. A previous episode details his fate. A year after that, Vincenza, named for her deceased brother, was the fourth child born to my grandparents. And two years after that, in 1920, my father's second oldest brother, Nick, left for America.

The years 1920 to 1940 saw my father live off the land, marry my mother Angela Spano in 1931, and have four girls and one boy, me. In 1933 he too was drafted into the Italian Army; he served in North Africa for a short time before he was medically discharged when he contracted malaria.

In 1940, at the age of 31, while my mother was pregnant with me, my father left for America, stowing away illegally on a ship, then living and working underground in New York City until he joined the US Army in April of 1942, serving for three years, and becoming a naturalized US citizen. At war's end, he sent for my mother, my older sister, and me. Three of my older sisters had died during the six years that my mother and father lived apart. Strangely, although my mother was vocal and emotional lamenting the loss of her three daughters for the rest of her life, my father never spoke of it to me.

For the next 44 years my father lived the American dream. He was self-employed until 1954, selling ice, kerosene and coal. Then, for the next 19 years he worked as a doorman in Manhattan. He retired in 1973, and died in 1990.

My memories of my father are that he was a very strict and harsh parent. Outside the home, however, he was gregarious and fun-loving, with many friends. Inside our home, though, my parents were constantly arguing. My sisters and I are pretty much in agreement that we do not like to argue or fight with our spouses or any others because of all the fighting we saw while we were growing up. My older sister, by the way, tells me that most of the fighting between my parents was about me. Usually it was because my father thought my mother was too over-protective. I suppose my father wanted me to be less timid than I was.

Have I grown up to be my father's son and how would he describe me today? Well, I believe he would tell me that I have not been strict enough in raising my children. I take it to mean I should have been less sensitive. For instance, when my first child, a boy, was born, I did not name him after my father, as our regional custom dictates. As a result my father purposely chose to distance himself from my son. The fact that I named him after myself, and my father-in-law coincidentally had the same first name only exacerbated the situation.

Finally, my father's description of me would be made in the context of what a father's role and behavior was supposed to be in Italy. My parenting was done in the context of being raised and educated in the US. For many years, both as a child and as a young adult I was torn between two different cultures. There is no question that I loved my father and that he loved me; however, he was raised in another world, literally. Since his passing in 1990, I have tried many times to talk to him. So far I have not heard from him. If given the chance to spend just one minute to have him with me again here on earth, I would give him the hug I never gave him all my life and tell him simply that I loved him, I had always loved him, and I believe he would say the same to me. I would also tell him that I think that what he did in 1940 was nothing short of heroic.

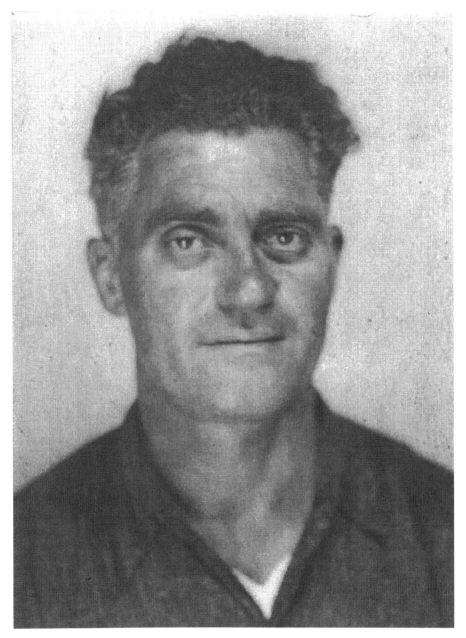

My Father, Massimiliano

Angela Rosa

"Angela Rosa," she always told us, was her full and given name at birth, not simply Angela, but Angela Rosa. She insisted on using her middle name.

Angela Rosa, my mother, must have been a real beauty when she was a young woman. I remember her as an old, graying, slightly over-weight woman. The earliest photograph I have of her is her wedding picture. She was twenty-two years old, the same age as my father, and that particular photo hints at her beautiful features: the dark brown, wavy hair, large brown eyes set above those high cheek-bones on that smooth, olive skin.

I suppose one could say she did not live a remarkable life. She had no formal education beyond first grade. Her accomplishments were those of a dutiful wife and mother to six children, five girls and one boy. The male child arrived after four girls had been born to her hus-band Massimiliano and herself. As a matter of fact, Massimiliano was in America at the time of my birth, having left Angela and the four girls while she was three months pregnant. It was probably a year or two before he learned that Angela had finally given him a son. The war in Europe caused many communications difficulties, and it wasn't until the war ended, and he had become a naturalized American citizen that he saw his family, including his six year old son, for the first time!

But those six years were extremely difficult for Angela, as depicted in a separate memoir in this book. Angela was thirty-seven years old when she first set foot on American soil. She learned the English language and studied and passed the citizenship test six years after her arrival in this country. She took great pride in becoming a naturalized American citizen.

Although my mother always spoke with a heavy Italian accent, she took great offense if anyone suggested she hadn't mastered the English language.

There is no doubt in my mind that I was the greatest joy in her life. While I was growing up she was constantly protecting me from my stern, harsh and demanding father. There were many quarrels between them and most of them seemed to be about me, and that fact has been vouched for by my older sister, Mary.

From the time I arrived in America until I left home for the military service it seemed that my mother was either taking me to doctors for one ailment or another, or caring for my annual bouts of influenza, bronchitis, ear aches and assorted other ailments. Always, *always*, she was there for me.

During my first year of teaching, while I was still single and just twenty-seven years old, I was hospitalized for three weeks, had major abdominal surgery, and missed two months of work. My mother, by herself, somehow navigated her way from the subway to the Long Island Railroad and from the railroad station by taxi to my bedside, more than fifty miles from her home in Astoria. She slept in my vacant bed and thanks to my roommate and kindly neighbors managed to come to the hospital every single day I was there.

Throughout my formative years, she encouraged me to be a better student, a better husband, a better person. Since I spent more time with my mother than with my father throughout my boyhood, she had of course the most influence on the person I became.

When I became a teacher, my mother burst with pride as she told friends and relatives, "My son is a teacher!" When I settled down and married at the age of thirty, I could literally see the calmness transformed in her.

In her mid-seventies, she showed the first signs of Alzheimer's disease, and it ultimately took its toll, destroying this woman who had been so full of vitality and energy. She spent the last 39 months of her life in a nursing home, barely a shell of her former self.

To me, my mother was everything a mother should be: loving, caring, kind, supportive, and generous. She was all of these things and much, much more. As depicted in a separate memoir, my father was very strict with me and on those all too often occurrences when he and I clashed, my mother somehow always managed to temper his harshness with gentleness.

I miss her.

Angela Rosa

My Grandfather, My Namesake

It's funny, the things we remember. My father's father, Francesco Tassielli, after whom I was named, lived to the ripe old age of ninety-seven. "Noo-noon," which is the southern Italian name for Grandpa, lived a full life. He was born and lived most of his life in the small, agrarian village of Sannicandro, located just outside the port city of Bari in southeastern Italy. As was the case for most boys his age, my grandfather left school after the first grade and went to work the land with his father. The meager wages and depressing poverty enveloped most of the residents of that region, as well as much of southern Italy, and that led to the mass migration of millions of men who sought work and the opportunity for a better life in other countries.

My grandfather went to Greece as a teenager and, strapping and strong individual that he was, he was able to withstand the rigors of physical labor handily. (Actually, his willingness and ability to work long and hard hours under the hot sun lasted until he was about ninety years old.) At any rate, his venture into Greece was short-lived as the work there was not as plentiful as he had thought. He returned to his village and a few years later married and began a family. Shortly thereafter, he made the first of several voyages to America, where he traveled as far west as Oregon and Washington State, helping to build the transcontinental railroad. He withstood the hard labor and often difficult prejudicial conditions, saved his money, and after almost two years, he returned to his family. On the third of these journeys to America, he was accompanied by his oldest son, my Uncle Vincenzo. This trip, however, was cut short when a letter arrived from Italy summoning both my grandfather

195

and his son to return to their homeland. World War I had broken out and the Italian Army was drafting its young men. The letter had a nasty tone in that it stated in no uncertain terms that if both men did not return they would forever forfeit their Italian citizenship and thus not be permitted a return to their family.

Within months of his arrival, subsequent induction and participation in the war, my uncle was wounded in battle. My grandfather and grandmother received word of his hospitalization and were offered the opportunity to travel hundreds of miles, where they could visit their son. Upon their arrival they were shocked to find an empty bed and given the tragic news that their son had succumbed to his wounds. My grandfather collapsed upon hearing this. The year was 1917 and my Uncle Vincenzo was twenty-one years old.

The years that followed saw my grandfather's second son, my Uncle Nick, and then his third son, my father Massimiliano, also leave Italy for a better life in America. It wasn't until 1964, when he was ninety-five years old, that he returned to America for the final time. His fourth child, my Aunt Vincenza, accompanied him on this final journey to reunite with her husband, two sons and a daughter. Because I was not quite six years old when I left Italy in 1946, my only memories of my grandfather were after 1964. By then he was stooped over and his memory was beginning to fade. He insisted, however, on smoking either his pipe or his cigar every day.

And so I come to the clearest memory I have of my grandfather. By 1964, he had been widowed about a dozen years and apparently still pined for female companionship. One day, as I passed by his cot where he had been resting, he suddenly sat up and asked me to come closer to him. As I did so, he took a one dollar bill out of his shirt pocket and pressed it into the palm of my hand. He asked me to go out and secure the services of a woman for him. Although his request embarrassed me somewhat, I maintained my poise and politely returned the bill to his shirt pocket. After rubbing the woolen skull cap he wore constantly and informing him of my refusal to comply with his request, he proceeded to rock back and forth on his cot while simultaneously letting out a scream of invectives (in Italian of course) that I dare not repeat. I was both amazed and amused. It's funny the things we remember.

All these years later, when I think of my grandfather, I hope that I have inherited some of his genes.

Francesco Tassielli

Sannicandro di Bari

Sannicandro di Bari is a small town whose population is currently approximately 9,000. It is located six miles from the port city of Bari, in the region known as Puglia, in the southeastern section of Italy. Its history goes back to the Peucetians, an ancient population that settled in the area in the seventh century BC.

In the seventh century AD a group of monks built a small church in the area and dedicated it to Saint Nicandro, a Christian from Crete who was martyred seven centuries earlier. From the time of his death people from the countryside gravitated to the church and it began to grow like a circle around the church. Over the years Saint Nicandro evolved until it became known by its current name of Sannicandro. In the tenth century the Byzantines ordered the building of a fortress to protect the town from invaders. As a result the small town increased in population as people from nearby villages came to Sannicandro to escape from the ravages of foreign invaders.

Rather than cite the many occupiers of the area, beginning with the Roman militia in the first century BC, suffice it to say that there have been quite a few since the time of Christ, and I'll bring the reader up to the twentieth century. The two world wars were very hard on the population of Sannicandro, both in deaths and emigration resulting from the feudal system of land ownership. Also, 1918 was especially difficult due to the Spanish Influenza which ravaged all of Europe; its toll was in the millions throughout the continent, and my maternal grandmother, Maria Volpe, was one of its victims; she was forty-five years old.

On the night of June 25, 1943, during the Second World War, the Royal Air Force of Britain bombed Sannicandro, resulting in ninety-five deaths. The reason for the bombing was never made clear.

Today, Sannicandro is still mainly agricultural, producing a heavy-bodied olive oil that contains the bitter taste of an endless hard toil.

Since I left Sannicandro at the age of five, in 1946, I have returned several times. The first time I returned was 1968, and modernization had begun, although many households still had only cold running water, and telephones in the home were few and far between. The last time I was there was 2002, and the modern age had arrived; there were cars everywhere. The narrow streets that were meant for horse and wagons were now traversed and filled with automobiles, their sounds a constant roar throughout the center of the town.

I sometimes wonder what my father or either of my two grandfathers who left for America for the first time in the late 19th century would think of Sannicandro as it is now in 2012.

Tassielli and Spano Family Trees

At some point during the writing of these memoirs I decided to include a family tree from both sides of my family. Getting all the pertinent facts has been a challenge, to say the least and there have been positive as well as negative aspects to this endeavor.

First, the positive: I've had to contact all of my first cousins and some of their children and their friendly, open attitude has definitely been a help, particularly on those occasions where I had to ask some awkward and uncomfortable questions. To all my cousins and their children: Thank you for providing me with all the information I needed! I always enjoyed speaking to each and every one of you!

As for the negative: A perusal of the two trees will readily inform the reader as to the magnitude of this project. I believe that only if one were to pursue such a project could he/she fully appreciate the complexity of the task. Thanks to the patience and expertise of Christine Fiore Hecht, I was able to sort out all the dates and pertinent facts and achieve a high degree of satisfaction upon its completion. A disclaimer: the mountains of paperwork accumulated during this project may have resulted in an incorrect year on some, hopefully, very few occasions. For those mistakes, please accept my apology.

Other ponderous decisions had to be considered as well, and they are as follows:

Should I include geographic location of marriages and births?

Should I include year of divorce?

Should I include country of birth for some spouses?

Perhaps the biggest questions I had to resolve were the listing of the first names of many of my relatives. This question requires some explanation: The given name (the name on their birth certificate) is very often not the name by which they are known throughout their lives. An Italian nickname is often used, a Baresi nickname is sometimes used, or an American nickname is used. Here are some examples:

A birth certificate listing Francesco becomes Franchino or Franco in Italian, Frongeen (phonetic spelling) in Sannicandresi, Frank or Frankie in English, and sometimes Cheech in all of the above.

Giovanni becomes Nino in dialect and John in English, and of course all of the English variations of John: Johnny, Jack, etc.

Luigi become Gene in dialect, and Louis, Louie, or Lou in English.

My decision after conversations with several of my cousins brought me to the conclusion that for the sake of consistency if nothing else I have chosen to use the name that is on the birth certificate on the Tassielli and Spano Family Trees. Hopefully, that consistent approach will result in some degree of clarity.

Finally, for the family tree on the Tassielli side I was able to go all the way back to my father's (Massimiliano) father's (Francesco) father's (Vincenzo) father, Francesco. Another way to express it is to say it's my father's great-grandfather, or my great-great-grandfather. I was able to go that far back because my paternal grandfather was an only son with two sisters, and his first-born son was Vincent. I was able to go that far back because I made the assumption that the Southern Italian tradition of naming children was followed, which is really not too great a leap of faith. Logic, or tradition, gave me enough of a comfort level to do so. The years of birth, however, are unknown.

As for the Spano side of my family, that is, my mother's side, there is one bit of information that from time to time has surfaced over the years, and it is this: My mother's father, Vito Antonio Spano, and my mother's mother, Maria Volpe Spano, having had three children, all girls, my mother being the youngest, had a fourth child, a boy; she suffered a stroke either during this pregnancy or shortly after giving birth, which partially paralyzed her for the next five years, until she died at age forty-five, in 1918. As a direct result of her disabling stroke, she was unable to give the child breast milk or other necessary nourishments, and he died shortly after birth. Assuming the infant was given a name, which would have been his paternal grandfather's name, I would at the very least be able to add the name not only of my mother's sole male sibling, but I would also be able to add the name of her paternal grandfather to the Spano family tree. However, in recent conversations with several of my oldest living cousins I have not been able to get verification of these facts from anyone other than my oldest sister, Mary. Therefore, my mother's family tree must begin with her father.

Descendants of Francesco Tassielli

Generation 1

1. **FRANCESCO[1] TASSIELLI** was born in 1810 in Sannicandro, Bari, Italy. He died date Unknown in Sannicandro, Bari, Italy.

Francesco Tassielli had the following child:

2.   i.   VINCENZO[2] TASSIELLI was born in 1840 in Sannicandro, Bari, Italy. He died date Unknown in Sannicandro, Bari, Italy. He married GRAZIA LAURA ZUCCARO. She was born date Unknown in Unknown. She died date Unknown in Unknown.

Generation 2

2. **VINCENZO[2] TASSIELLI** (Francesco[1]) was born in 1840 in Sannicandro, Bari, Italy. He died date Unknown in Sannicandro, Bari, Italy. He married **GRAZIA LAURA ZUCCARO**. She was born date Unknown in Unknown. She died date Unknown in Unknown.

Vincenzo Tassielli and Grazia Laura Zuccaro had the following children:

3.   i.   FRANCESCO[3] TASSIELLI was born in 1869 in Sannicandro, Bari, Italy. He died in 1966 in Queens, NY. He married Maria Carmela DeCicco in 1894 in Sannicandro, Bari, Italy. She was born in 1876 in Sannicandro, Bari, Italy. She died in 1954 in Sannicandro, Bari, Italy.

     i.   CARMINA TASSIELLI was born date Unknown in Sannicandro, Bari, Italy. She died date Unknown in Sannicandro, Bari, Italy. She married VITO FARELLA.

     ii.   MARIA GIUSEPPINA TASSIELLI was born date Unknown in Sannicandro, Bari, Italy. She died date Unknown in Sannicandro, Bari, Italy. She married GIUSEPPE VIAPIANO. He was born in Cassano, Italy.

Generation 3

3.   **FRANCESCO³ TASSIELLI** (Vincenzo², Francesco¹) was born in 1869 in Sannicandro, Bari, Italy. He died in 1966 in Queens, NY. He married Maria Carmela
DeCicco in 1894 in Sannicandro, Bari, Italy. She was born in 1876 in Sannicandro, Bari, Italy. She died in 1954 in Sannicandro, Bari, Italy.

Notes for Maria Carmela DeCicco:
She had two brothers, Vito Nicola DeCicco, who married Rosa (surname
unknown), and Giovanni DeCicco, who married Domenica (surname unknown),
and one sister, Vincenza DeCicco, who married a man named Michele Rizzi.

Francesco Tassielli and Maria Carmela DeCicco had the following children:

      i.   VINCENZO⁴ TASSIELLI was born in 1895 in Sannicandro, Bari,
           Italy. He died in 1916 in Italy.

           Notes for Vincenzo Tassielli:
           Killed in action, WW1

4.   ii.   NICOLA TASSIELLI was born in 1900 in Sannicandro, Bari, Italy.
           He died in 1990 in New Jersey. He married Anna Clarizio in 1928
           in Sannicandro, Bari, Italy. She was born in 1906 in Sannicandro,
           Bari, Italy. She died in 2003 in New Jersey.

5.   iii. MASSIMILIANO TASSIELLI was born in 1908 in Sannicandro,
           Bari, Italy. He died in 1990 in Coram, NY. He married Angela Rosa
           Spano, daughter of Vito Antonio Spano and Maria Volpe in 1931.
           She was born in 1909 in Sannicandro, Bari, Italy. She died in 1992
           in Nesconset, NY.

6.   iv. VINCENZA TASSIELLI was born in 1917 in Sannicandro, Bari,
           Italy. She married

           Giuseppe Chiechi in 1936 in Sannicandro, Bari, Italy. He was born
           in 1912 in
           Sannicandro, Bari, Italy. He died in 1999 in New York.

Generation 4

4. **NICOLA**[4] **TASSIELLI** (Francesco[3], Vincenzo[2], Francesco[1]) was born in 1900 in Sannicandro, Bari, Italy. He died in 1990 in New Jersey. He married Anna Clarizio in 1928 in Sannicandro, Bari, Italy. She was born in 1906 in Sannicandro, Bari, Italy. She died in 2003 in New Jersey.

Nicola Tassielli and Anna Clarizio had the following children:

7. i. MARIA[5] TASSIELLI was born in 1929 in New Jersey. She married Donald Longo in 1954 in New Jersey. He was born in 1928 in New York. He died in 2006 in New Jersey.

8. ii. VINCENZA TASSIELLI was born in 1932 in New Jersey. She married Walter Robert Speck in 1967 in New Jersey. He was born in 1934 in New Jersey.

9. iii. FRANCESCO TASSIELLI was born in 1935 in New Jersey. He married Barbara DiCarlis in 1962 in New Jersey. She was born in 1938 in New Jersey.

10. iv. OTTAVIO TASSIELLI was born in 1944 in New Jersey. He married Cynthia Wahl in 1979 in Arizona. She was born in 1957.

5. **MASSIMILIANO**[4] **TASSIELLI** (Francesco[3], Vincenzo[2], Francesco[1]) was born in 1908 in Sannicandro, Bari, Italy. He died in 1990 in Coram, NY. He married Angela Rosa Spano, daughter of Vito Antonio Spano and Maria Volpe in 1931. She was born in 1909 in Sannicandro, Bari, Italy. She died in 1992 in Nesconset, NY.

Massimiliano Tassielli and Angela Rosa Spano had the following children:

i. MARIA CARMELA[5] TASSIELLI was born in 1931 in Sannicandro, Bari, Italy. She died in 1944 in Sannicandro, Bari, Italy.

11. ii. MARIA TASSIELLI was born in 1934 in Sannicandro, Bari, Italy. She married Vito Stangarone in 1958 in New York. He was born in 1935 in Sannicandro, Bari, Italy.

Generation 4 (con't)

iii. GRAZIA TASSIELLI was born in 1936 in Sannicandro, Bari, Italy. She died in 1940 in Sannicandro, Bari, Italy.

vi. ANTONIA TASSIELLI was born in 1938 in Sannicandro, Bari, Italy. She died in 1940 in Sannicandro, Bari, Italy.

12. v. FRANCESCO TASSIELLI was born in 1940 in Sannicandro, Bari, Italy. He married Diane Tullo in 1970 in Queens, NY. She was born in 1947 in Queens, NY.

13. vi. GRAZIA TASSIELLI was born in 1947 in New York, NY. She married Harry Jackson in 1967 in New York. He was born in 1947. He died in 2012.

6. **VINCENZA**[4] **TASSIELLI** (Francesco[3], Vincenzo[2], Francesco[1]) was born in 1917 in Sannicandro, Bari, Italy. She married Giuseppe Chiechi in 1936 in Sannicandro, Bari, Italy. He was born in 1912 in Sannicandro, Bari, Italy. He died in 1999 in New York.

Giuseppe Chiechi and Vincenza Tassielli had the following children:

14. i. ROSELLA[5] CHIECHI was born in 1937 in Sannicandro, Bari, Italy. She married Vittorio Cassano in 1965 in New York. He was born in 1936 in Castellaneta, Italy.

15. ii. GIOVANNI CHIECHI was born in 1940 in Sannicandro, Bari, Italy. He married Assunta

Carbonara in 1968 in New York. She was born in 1944 in Naples, Italy.

16. iii. FRANCESCO CHIECHI was born in 1947 in Sannicandro, Bari, Italy. He married Dina Baccillieri in 1974 in New York. She was born in 1949.

Generation 5

7. **MARIA⁵ TASSIELLI** (Nicola⁴, Francesco³, Vincenzo², Francesco¹) was born in 1929 in New Jersey. She married Donald Longo in 1954 in New Jersey. He was born in 1928 in New York. He died in 2006 in New Jersey.

Donald Longo and Maria Tassielli had the following children:

17. i.   DONALD⁶ LONGO was born in 1955 in New Jersey. He died in 2001 in New Jersey. He married JANE JACKSON. She was born in 1955.

18. ii. JOANNE LONGO was born in 1960 in New Jersey. She married John Fagan in 1986 in New Jersey. He was born in 1958 in New Jersey.

19. iii. PETER LONGO was born in 1964 in New Jersey. He married (1) SHARON DOYLE in 1986. She was born in 1964. He married (2) MICHELLE MCCARTNEY in 2007. She was born in 1970.

20. iv. MARY JEAN LONGO was born in 1969 in New Jersey. She married Frank Boensch in 1999 in New Jersey. He was born in 1967 in Columbus, Ohio.

8. **VINCENZA⁵ TASSIELLI** (Nicola⁴, Francesco³, Vincenzo², Francesco¹) was born in 1932 in New Jersey. She married Walter Robert Speck in 1967 in New Jersey. He was born in 1934 in New Jersey.

Walter Robert Speck and Vincenza Tassielli had the following children:

21. i.   ROBERT CHRISTOPHER⁶ SPECK was born in 1968 in New Jersey. He married Olga Nikiforova in 2002 in New Jersey. She was born in 1974 in Ukraine.

22. ii. WALTER GREGORY SPECK was born in 1970 in New Jersey. He married Jeannette Rooney in 1997 in New Jersey. She was born in 1970.

iii. ERIC SPECK was born in 1975 in New Jersey. He married Allison Berkeley in 2009 in Texas. She was born in Texas.

Generation 5 (con't)

9. **FRANCESCO**[5] **TASSIELLI** (Nicola[4], Francesco[3], Vincenzo[2], Francesco[1]) was born in 1935 in New Jersey. He married Barbara DiCarlis in 1962 in New Jersey. She was born in 1938 in New Jersey.

    Francesco Tassielli and Barbara DiCarlis had the following children:

    23. i. ANNA MARIA[6] TASSIELLI was born in 1963 in New Jersey. She married Edward Kalinowski in 1992 in New Jersey. He was born in 1960.

    24. ii. NICHOLAS TASSIELLI was born in 1964 in New Jersey. He married Gina Leonardis in 1991 in New Jersey. She was born in 1965.

    25. iii. STEPHANIE TASSIELLI was born in 1969 in New Jersey. She married Michael Kirchner in 1997 in New Jersey. He was born in 1966.

10. **OTTAVIO**[5] **TASSIELLI** (Nicola[4], Francesco[3], Vincenzo[2], Francesco[1]) was born in 1944 in New Jersey. He married Cynthia Wahl in 1979 in Arizona. She was born in 1957.

    Ottavio Tassielli and Cynthia Wahl were divorced in 1994.
    Ottavio Tassielli and Cynthia Wahl had the following children:

    i. NICOLE[6] TASSIELLI was born in 1983 in Arizona.

    ii. DANIELLE TASSIELLI was born in 1986 in Arizona.

11. **MARIA**[5] **TASSIELLI** (Massimiliano[4], Francesco[3], Vincenzo[2], Francesco[1]) was born in 1934 in Sannicandro, Bari, Italy. She married Vito Stangarone in 1958 in New York. He was born in 1935 in Sannicandro, Bari, Italy.

    Vito Stangarone and Maria Tassielli had the following children:

    26. i. UMBERTO[6] STANGARONE was born in 1958 in New York. He married Jean Scaglione in 1989 in New Jersey. She was born in 1962.

  i. CONSTANCE STANGARONE was born in 1959 in New York.

  ii. MAXIMILLIAN STANGARONE was born in 1961 in New York.

  i. ANGELA STANGARONE was born in 1963 in New York.

27. v. SUSANNE STANGARONE was born in 1963 in New York. She married Robert Galvin in 2000 in New York. He was born in 1958 in New York.

28. vi. MARTIN STANGARONE was born in 1968 in New York. He married Jodi Rheingold in 1997 in New York. She was born in 1968.

12. **FRANCESCO[5] TASSIELLI** (Massimiliano[4], Francesco[3], Vincenzo[2], Francesco[1]) was born in 1940 in Sannicandro, Bari, Italy. He married Diane Tullo in 1970 in Queens, NY. She was born in 1947 in Queens, NY.

Francesco Tassielli and Diane Tullo had the following children:
  i. FRANK[6] TASSIELLI was born in 1972 in Smithtown, NY.

29. ii. SHARON TASSIELLI was born in 1975 in Smithtown, NY. She married Joseph Annese in 2001 in Miller Place, NY. He was born in 1975 in New York.

13. **GRAZIA[5] TASSIELLI** (Massimiliano[4], Francesco[3], Vincenzo[2], Francesco[1]) was born in 1947 in New York, NY. She married Harry Jackson in 1967 in New York. He was born in 1947. He died in 2012.

Harry Jackson and Grazia Tassielli had the following children:
  i. JOSEPH[6] JACKSON was born in 1968.

  ii. KERRY JACKSON was born in 1969.

30. iii. LINDA JACKSON was born in 1971. She married Jeff White in 2001. He was born in 1963.

  vi. MICHAEL JACKSON was born in 1981.

Generation 5 (con't)

14. **ROSELLA**[5] **CHIECHI** (Vincenza[4] Tassielli, Francesco[3] Tassielli, Vincenzo[2] Tassielli, Francesco[1] Tassielli) was born in 1937 in Sannicandro, Bari, Italy. She married Vittorio Cassano in 1965 in New York. He was born in 1936 in Castellaneta, Italy.

Vittorio Cassano and Rosella Chiechi had the following children:

   31.   i.   CLAIRE[6] CASSANO was born in 1966 in New York. She married George Mangione in 1992 in New York. He was born in 1965 in New York.

   32.   ii.   CYNTHIA CASSANO was born in 1967 in New York. She married Luciano DiNorcia in 1994 in New York. He was born in 1965 in Italy.

       iii.   ROSEANNE CASSANO was born in 1971 in New York. She married Scott Marn in 2008 in New York.

15. **GIOVANNI**[5] **CHIECHI** (Vincenza[4] Tassielli, Francesco[3] Tassielli, Vincenzo[2] Tassielli, Francesco[1] Tassielli) was born in 1940 in Sannicandro, Bari, Italy. He married Assunta Carbonara in 1968 in New York. She was born in 1944 in Naples, Italy.

Giovanni Chiechi and Assunta Carbonara had the following children:

   33.   i.   JOSEPH[6] CHIECHI was born in 1969 in New York. He died in 2012 in Connecticut. He married Susan Lattanzi in 2007 in Connecticut. She was born in 1969.

   34.   ii.   JOHN VITO CHIECHI was born in 1970 in New York. He married Pamela Orrichio in 2006 in Connecticut. She was born in 1973.

       iii.   FRANK CHIECHI was born in 1977 in Connecticut. He married Christina Dorazio in 2009 in New York. She was born in 1980.

       iv.   ERICA CHIECHI was born in 1979 in Connecticut. She married Miles Potts in 2011 in New York. He was born in 1973.

16. **FRANCESCO**[5] **CHIECHI** (Vincenza[4] Tassielli, Francesco[3] Tassielli, Vincenzo[2] Tassielli, Francesco[1] Tassielli) was born in 1947 in Sannicandro, Bari, Italy. He married Dina Baccillieri in 1974 in New York. She was born in 1949.

Francesco Chiechi and Dina Baccillieri had the following children:

      i.   JOSEPH[6] CHIECHI was born in 1975.

      ii.   MICHAEL CHIECHI was born in 1980.

     iii. CYNTHIA CHIECHI was born in 1983.

Generation 6

17. **DONALD**[6] **LONGO** (Maria[5] Tassielli, Nicola[4] Tassielli, Francesco[3] Tassielli, Vincenzo[2] Tassielli, Francesco[1] Tassielli) was born in 1955 in New Jersey. He died in 2001 in New Jersey. He married **JANE JACKSON**. She was born in 1955.

Donald Longo and Jane Jackson were divorced in 2002.
Donald Longo and Jane Jackson had the following children:

      i.   MICHAEL[7] LONGO was born in 1982 in New Jersey.

      ii.   NICHOLAS LONGO was born in 1984 in New Jersey.

18. **JOANNE**[6] **LONGO** (Maria[5] Tassielli, Nicola[4] Tassielli, Francesco[3] Tassielli, Vincenzo[2] Tassielli, Francesco[1] Tassielli) was born in 1960 in New Jersey. She married John Fagan in 1986 in New Jersey. He was born in 1958 in New Jersey.

John Fagan and Joanne Longo had the following children:

      i.   JOHN[7] FAGAN was born in 1991 in New Jersey.

      ii.   JACQUELINE FAGAN was born in 1993 in New Jersey.

     iii. JILLIAN FAGAN was born in 1995 in New Jersey.

Generation 6 (con't)

19. **PETER**[6] **LONGO** (Maria[5] Tassielli, Nicola[4] Tassielli, Francesco[3] Tassielli, Vincenzo[2] Tassielli, Francesco[1] Tassielli) was born in 1964 in New Jersey. He married (1) **SHARON DOYLE** in 1986. She was born in 1964. He married (2) **MICHELLE MCCARTNEY** in 2007. She was born in 1970.

Peter Longo and Sharon Doyle were divorced in 2001.
Peter Longo and Sharon Doyle had the following children:
      i.   SAMANTHA[7] LONGO was born in 1985.

      ii.   LEIGH ANN LONGO was born in 1988.

      iii.   PETER LONGO was born in 1993.

20. **MARY JEAN**[6] **LONGO** (Maria[5] Tassielli, Nicola[4] Tassielli, Francesco[3] Tassielli, Vincenzo[2] Tassielli, Francesco[1] Tassielli) was born in 1969 in New Jersey. She married Frank Boensch in 1999 in New Jersey. He was born in 1967 in Columbus, Ohio.

Frank Boensch and Mary Jean Longo had the following children:
      i.   SOFIA[7] BOENSCH was born in 2003 in New Jersey.

      ii.   FRANK BOENSCH was born in 2007 in New Jersey.

21 **ROBERT CHRISTOPHER**[6] **SPECK** (Vincenza[5] Tassielli, Nicola[4] Tassielli, Francesco[3] Tassielli, Vincenzo[2] Tassielli, Francesco[1] Tassielli) was born in 1968 in New Jersey. He married Olga Nikiforova in 2002 in New Jersey. She was born in 1974 in Ukraine.

Robert Christopher Speck and Olga Nikiforova had the following children:
      i.   STEVEN[7] SPECK was born in 2004.

      ii.   GARY SPECK was born in 2008.

22. **WALTER GREGORY**[6] **SPECK** (Vincenza[5] Tassielli, Nicola[4] Tassielli, Francesco[3] Tassielli, Vincenzo[2] Tassielli, Francesco[1] Tassielli) was born in 1970 in

New Jersey. He married Jeannette Rooney in 1997 in New Jersey. She was born in 1970.

Walter Gregory Speck and Jeannette Rooney had the following children:

i.   LAUREN[7] SPECK was born in 2001.

ii. CAROLINE SPECK was born in 2004.

iii. COURTNEY SPECK was born in 2007.

23. **ANNA MARIA**[6] **TASSIELLI** (Francesco[5], Nicola[4], Francesco[3], Vincenzo[2], Francesco[1]) was born in 1963 in New Jersey. She married Edward Kalinowski in 1992 in New Jersey. He was born in 1960.

Edward Kalinowski and Anna Maria Tassielli had the following children:

i.   CHRISTINA[7] KALINOWSKI was born in 1995 in New Jersey.

ii. CASSANDRA KALINOWSKI was born in 1997 in New Jersey.

iii. THOMAS KALINOWSKI was born in 1999 in New Jersey.

Generation 6 (con't)

24. **NICHOLAS**[6] **TASSIELLI** (Francesco[5], Nicola[4], Francesco[3], Vincenzo[2], Francesco[1]) was born in 1964 in New Jersey. He married Gina Leonardis in 1991 in New Jersey. She was born in 1965.

Nicholas Tassielli and Gina Leonardis had the following children:
    i.   FRANK[7] TASSIELLI was born in 1993 in New Jersey.

    ii.   NICOLE TASSIELLI was born in 1996 in New Jersey.

25. **STEPHANIE**[6] **TASSIELLI** (Francesco[5], Nicola[4], Francesco[3], Vincenzo[2], Francesco[1]) was born in 1969 in New Jersey. She married Michael Kirchner in 1997 in New Jersey. He was born in 1966.

Michael Kirchner and Stephanie Tassielli had the following children:
    i.   MICHAEL[7] KIRCHNER was born in 2000 in New Jersey.

    ii.   ELLA KIRCHNER was born in 2003 in New Jersey.

26. **UMBERTO**[6] **STANGARONE** (Maria[5] Tassielli, Massimiliano[4] Tassielli, Francesco[3] Tassielli, Vincenzo[2] Tassielli, Francesco[1] Tassielli) was born in 1958 in New York. He married Jean Scaglione in 1989 in New Jersey. She was born in 1962.

Umberto Stangarone and Jean Scaglione had the following children:
    i.   DEAN[7] STANGARONE was born in 1992 in New Jersey.

    ii.   ALEX STANGARONE was born in 1996 in New Jersey.

27. **SUSANNE**[6] **STANGARONE** (Maria[5] Tassielli, Massimiliano[4] Tassielli, Francesco[3] Tassielli, Vincenzo[2] Tassielli, Francesco[1] Tassielli) was born in 1963 in New York. She married Robert Galvin in 2000 in New York. He was born in 1958 in New York.

Robert Galvin and Susanne Stangarone had the following child:
    i.   JACK[7] GALVIN was born in 2000 in New Jersey.

28. **MARTIN**[6] **STANGARONE** (Maria[5] Tassielli, Massimiliano[4] Tassielli, Francesco[3] Tassielli, Vincenzo[2] Tassielli, Francesco[1] Tassielli) was born in 1968 in New York. He married Jodi Rheingold in 1997 in New York. She was born in 1968.

Martin Stangarone and Jodi Rheingold had the following children:
  i. ABIGAIL[7] STANGARONE was born in 2001 in New York.

  ii. CHARLIE STANGARONE was born in 2005 in New York.

29. **SHARON**[6] **TASSIELLI** (Francesco[5], Massimiliano[4], Francesco[3], Vincenzo[2], Francesco[1]) was born in 1975 in Smithtown, NY. She married Joseph Annese in 2001 in Miller Place, NY. He was born in 1975 in New York.

Joseph Annese and Sharon Tassielli had the following children:
  i. ALEXA[7] ANNESE was born in 2002 in Queens, NY.

  ii. NICHOLAS ANNESE was born in 2006 in Queens, NY.

  iii. DANIELLE ANNESE was born in 2007 in Smithtown, NY.

30. **LINDA**[6] **JACKSON** (Grazia[5] Tassielli, Massimiliano[4] Tassielli, Francesco[3] Tassielli, Vincenzo[2] Tassielli, Francesco[1] Tassielli) was born in 1971. She married Jeff White in 2001. He was born in 1963.

Jeff White and Linda Jackson had the following children:
  i. EMILY[7] WHITE was born in 2003.

  ii. ALLYSON WHITE was born in 2004.

31. **CLAIRE**[6] **CASSANO** (Rosella[5] Chiechi, Vincenza[4] Tassielli, Francesco[3] Tassielli, Vincenzo[2] Tassielli, Francesco[1] Tassielli) was born in 1966 in New York. She married George Mangione in 1992 in New York. He was born in 1965 in New York.

George Mangione and Claire Cassano had the following children:
  i. MATTHEW[7] MANGIONE was born in 1995 in New York.

Generation 6 (con't)

    ii.   MARISSA MANGIONE was born in 1998 in New York.

    iii.   ALEXA MANGIONE was born in 2002 in New York.

32. **CYNTHIA**[6] **CASSANO** (Rosella[5] Chiechi, Vincenza[4] Tassielli, Francesco[3] Tassielli, Vincenzo[2] Tassielli, Francesco[1] Tassielli) was born in 1967 in New York. She married Luciano DiNorcia in 1994 in New York. He was born in 1965 in Italy.

Luciano DiNorcia and Cynthia Cassano had the following children:
    i.   CHRISTINA[7] DINORCIA was born in 1996 in New York.

    ii.   MICHAEL DINORCIA was born in 1998 in New York.

33. **JOSEPH**[6] **CHIECHI** (Giovanni[5], Vincenza[4] Tassielli, Francesco[3] Tassielli, Vincenzo[2] Tassielli, Francesco[1] Tassielli) was born in 1969 in New York. He died in 2012 in Connecticut. He married Susan Lattanzi in 2007 in Connecticut. She was born in 1969.

Joseph Chiechi and Susan Lattanzi had the following children:
    i.   CHRISTIAN[7] CHIECHI was born in 2008 in Connecticut.

    ii.   ERICA CHIECHI was born in 2010 in Connecticut.

34. **JOHN VITO**[6] **CHIECHI** (Giovanni[5], Vincenza[4] Tassielli, Francesco[3] Tassielli, Vincenzo[2] Tassielli, Francesco[1] Tassielli) was born in 1970 in New York. He married Pamela Orrichio in 2006 in Connecticut. She was born in 1973.

John Vito Chiechi and Pamela Orrichio had the following children:
    i.   JONATHAN[7] CHIECHI was born in 2007 in Connecticut.

    ii.   GABRIELLA CHIECHI was born in 2011 in Connecticut.

35. **ERICA**[6] **CHIECHI** (Giovanni[5], Vincenza[4] Tassielli, Francesco[3] Tassielli, Vincenzo[2] Tassielli, Francesco[1] Tassielli) was born in 1979 in Connecticut. She married Miles Potts in 2011 in New York. He was born in 1973.

Erica Chiechi and Miles Potts had the following children:
    i.   Joseph Potts was born in 2012.

Descendants of Vito Antonio Spano

Generation 1

2.   **VITO ANTONIO**[1] **SPANO** was born in 1867 in Grumo, Italy. He died in 1954 in Sannicandro, Bari, Italy. He married (1) **MARIA VOLPE,** daughter of Rocco Volpe and Angela Rosa Rizzi in 1896 in Sannicandro, Bari, Italy. She was born in 1873 in Sannicandro, Bari, Italy. She died in 1918 in Sannicandro, Bari, Italy. He married (2) **MARIA RACANELLI** date Unknown. She was born in 1884. She died in 1953.

Notes for Maria Volpe:

Her father was Rocco Volpe and her mother, Angela Rosa Rizzi. Maria had two siblings: sister Maddalena Volpe Racanelli and brother Rocco Volpe.

Vito Antonio Spano and Maria Volpe had the following children:

2.   i.   CATERINA[2] SPANO was born in 1898 in Sannicandro, Bari, Italy. She died in 1981 in New York. She married Nicola Manchisi in 1919 in Sannicandro, Bari, Italy. He was born in 1893 in Sannicandro, Bari, Italy. He died in 1970 in New York.

3.   ii. DONATA SPANO was born in 1902 in Sannicandro, Bari, Italy. She died in 1988 in New York. She married Luigi Racanelli in 1925 in Sannicandro, Bari, Italy. He was born in 1893 in Sannicandro, Bari, Italy. He died in 1975 in New York.

4.   iii. ANGELA ROSA SPANO was born in 1909 in Sannicandro, Bari, Italy. She died in 1992 in Nesconset, NY. She married Massimiliano Tassielli, son of Francesco Tassielli and Maria Carmela DeCicco in 1931. He was born in 1908 in Sannicandro, Bari, Italy. He died in 1990 in Coram, NY.

Generation 2

3.   **CATERINA**[2] **SPANO** (Vito Antonio[1]) was born in 1898 in Sannicandro, Bari, Italy. She died in 1981 in New York. She married Nicola Manchisi in 1919 in Sannicandro, Bari, Italy. He was born in 1893 in Sannicandro, Bari, Italy. He died in 1970 in New York.

Nicola Manchisi and Caterina Spano had the following children:

3.   i.   GENNARO[3] MANCHISI was born in 1920 in Sannicandro, Bari, Italy. He died in 2007 in Florida. He married Angela Racanelli in 1944 in New York. She was born in 1922 in Sannicandro, Bari, Italy. She died in 2009 in Florida.

     ii.   MARIA MANCHISI was born in 1926 in Sannicandro, Bari, Italy. She died in 2010 in New York. She married (1) GIUSEPPE LABI-ANCA in 1946 in Sannicandro, Bari, Italy. He was born in 1925 in Sannicandro, Bari, Italy. He died in 1947 in Sannicandro, Bari, Italy. She married (2) MICHELE DIMARTINO in 1956 in Italy. He was born in 1931 in Italy.

4.   iii.   VITO ANTONIO MANCHISI was born in 1930 in Sannicandro, Bari, Italy. He married Giuseppina Lucarelli in 1958 in Sannicandro, Bari, Italy. She was born in 1939 in Sannicandro, Bari, Italy.

4.   **DONATA**[2] **SPANO** (Vito Antonio[1]) was born in 1902 in Sannicandro, Bari, Italy. She died in 1988 in New York. She married Luigi Racanelli in 1925 in Sannicandro, Bari, Italy. He was born in 1893 in Sannicandro, Bari, Italy. He died in 1975 in New York.

Luigi Racanelli and Donata Spano had the following children:

8.   i.   ANGELANTONIO[3] RACANELLI was born in 1926 in Sannicandro, Bari, Italy. He died in 2004. He married Rosa Simone in 1951 in Sannicandro, Bari, Italy. She was born in 1932 in Sannicandro, Bari, Italy. She died in 2000 in New York.

9.   ii.   VITO RACANELLI was born in 1928 in Sannicandro, Bari, Italy. He married Carmela Racanelli in 1952 in New York. She was born in 1932 in Sannicandro, Bari, Italy.

She died in 2002 in New York.

8.   iii.   FRANCESCO RACANELLI was born in 1931 in Sannicandro, Bari, Italy. He married Donatella Iacobellis in 1963 in Sannicandro, Bari, Italy. She was born in 1936 in Sannicandro, Bari, Italy.

9.   iv.   ROSALIE RACANELLI was born in 1933 in Sannicandro, Bari, Italy. She married Domenico Stea in 1958 in Sannicandro, Bari, Italy. He was born in 1928 in Sannicandro, Bari, Italy.

10.   v.   ROCCO RACANELLI was born in 1935 in Sannicandro, Bari, Italy. He married Lorraine Orera in 1975 in New York. She was born in 1938 in New York.

11.   vi.   MARIA RACANELLI was born in 1940 in Sannicandro, Bari, Italy. She married Gino Stea in 1964 in New York. He was born in 1937 in Sannicandro, Bari, Italy.

12.   vii.   ANGELA RACANELLI was born in 1944 in Sannicandro, Bari, Italy. She married Vito Mossa in 1967 in New York. He was born in 1939 in Sannicandro, Bari, Italy.

2.   **ANGELA ROSA**[2] **SPANO** (Vito Antonio[1]) was born in 1909 in Sannicandro, Bari, Italy. She died in 1992 in Nesconset, NY. She married Massimiliano Tassielli, son of Francesco Tassielli and Maria Carmela DeCicco in 1931. He was born in 1908 in Sannicandro, Bari, Italy. He died in 1990 in Coram, NY.

Massimiliano Tassielli and Angela Rosa Spano had the following children:

       iii.   MARIA CARMELA[3] TASSIELLI was born in 1931 in Sannicandro, Bari, Italy. She died in 1944 in Sannicandro, Bari, Italy.

12.   ii.   MARIA TASSIELLI was born in 1934 in Sannicandro, Bari, Italy. She married Vito Stangarone in 1958 in New York. He was born in 1935 in Sannicandro, Bari, Italy.

       i.   GRAZIA TASSIELLI was born in 1936 in Sannicandro, Bari, Italy. She died in 1940 in Sannicandro, Bari, Italy.

Generation 2 (con't)

ii.   ANTONIA TASSIELLI was born in 1938 in Sannicandro, Bari, Italy. She died in 1940 in Sannicandro, Bari, Italy.

iii.   FRANCESCO TASSIELLI was born in 1940 in Sannicandro, Bari, Italy. He married Diane Tullo in 1970 in Queens, NY. She was born in 1947 in Queens, NY.

iv.   GRAZIA TASSIELLI was born in 1947 in New York, NY. She married Harry Jackson in 1967 in New York. He was born in 1947.

Generation 3

5.   **GENNARO³ MANCHISI** (Caterina² Spano, Vito Antonio¹ Spano) was born in 1920 in Sannicandro, Bari, Italy. He died in 2007 in Florida. He married Angela Racanelli in 1944 in New York. She was born in 1922 in Sannicandro, Bari, Italy. She died in 2009 in Florida.

Gennaro Manchisi and Angela Racanelli had the following children:

2.   i.   NICOLA⁴ MANCHISI was born in 1945 in New York. He married (1) JOYCE GUTTERWELL in 1966 in New York. He married (2) LINDA PIZZINO in 1975 in Michigan. She was born in 1951 in Michigan.

3.   ii.   CATERINA MANCHISI was born in 1950 in New York. She married Tony Uanino in 1970 in New York. He was born in 1946 in New York.

19.   iii.   SERENA MANCHISI was born in 1953 in New York. She married William MacLellan in 1976 in New York. He was born in 1953.

20.   iv.   MARIA MANCHISI was born in 1955 in New York. She married Anthony Coleman in 1978. He was born in 1950.

v.   JOSEPH MANCHISI was born in 1963 in New York. He married (1) JO LYN ASHCRAFT in 1987. She was born in 1964. He married (2) TERRI HAMBURGER in 2001. She was born in 1972.

6. **VITO ANTONIO**[3] **MANCHISI** (Caterina[2] Spano, Vito Antonio[1] Spano) was born in 1930 in Sannicandro, Bari, Italy. He married Giuseppina Lucarelli in 1958 in Sannicandro, Bari, Italy. She was born in 1939 in Sannicandro, Bari, Italy.

Vito Antonio Manchisi and Giuseppina Lucarelli had the following children:

21.   i.   CATHERINE[4] MANCHISI was born in 1959 in New York. She married Thomas Englehardt in 1987 in New York. He was born in 1956.

22.   ii.   NICOLA MANCHISI was born in 1963 in New York. He married Maria Apostolidis in 2008 in New York. She was born in 1971.

23.   iii.   MARIANNE MANCHISI was born in 1970 in New York. She married James Smith in 2000 in New York. He was born in 1968.

24.   iv.   ANGELA MANCHISI was born in 1978 in New York. She married Salvatore Talluto in 2003 in New York. He was born in 1974.

7. **ANGELANTONIO**[3] **RACANELLI** (Donata[2] Spano, Vito Antonio[1] Spano) was born in 1926 in Sannicandro, Bari, Italy. He died in 2004. He married Rosa Simone in 1951 in Sannicandro, Bari, Italy. She was born in 1932 in Sannicandro, Bari, Italy. She died in 2000 in New York.

Angelantonio Racanelli and Rosa Simone had the following children:

25.   i.   LUIGI[4] RACANELLI was born in 1952 in Sannicandro, Bari, Italy. He married Roseanne Mosto in 1975. She was born in 1954.

26.   ii.   VINCENZO RACANELLI was born in 1953 in Sannicandro, Bari, Italy. He married Anna Barry in 1978 in New York. She was born in 1951 in Ireland. She died in 1996 in New York.

27.   iii.   DINO RACANELLI was born in 1962 in Sannicandro, Bari, Italy. He married Lillian DiBella in 1996 in New York. She was born in 1969.

8. **VITO**[3] **RACANELLI** (Donata[2] Spano, Vito Antonio[1] Spano) was born in 1928 in Sannicandro, Bari, Italy. He married Carmela Racanelli in 1952 in New York. She was born in 1932 in Sannicandro, Bari, Italy. She died in 2002 in New York.

Generation 3 (con't)

Vito Racanelli and Carmela Racanelli had the following children:

28. i. LUIGI[4] RACANELLI was born in 1954 in New York. He married Nancy Rufrano in 1986 in New York. She was born in 1955.

29. ii. JOSEPH RACANELLI was born in 1961 in New York. He married Kristine Dorritie in 1990 in New York. She was born in 1961 in New York.

30. iii. ANTHONY RACANELLI was born in 1967 in New York. He married Amalia Glickman in 1993 in New York. She was born in 1968.

31. iv. JOHN RACANELLI was born in 1969 in New York. He married Christine Grote in 1999 in New York. She was born in 1969.

9. **FRANCESCO**[3] **RACANELLI** (Donata[2] Spano, Vito Antonio[1] Spano) was born in 1931 in Sannicandro, Bari, Italy. He married Donatella Iacobellis in 1963 in Sannicandro, Bari, Italy. She was born in 1936 in Sannicandro, Bari, Italy.

Francesco Racanelli and Donatella Iacobellis had the following child:

32. i. LUIGI[4] RACANELLI was born in 1964 in Sannicandro, Bari, Italy. He married DANIELA DEPINTO. She was born in 1965 in Sannicandro, Bari, Italy.

10. **ROSALIE**[3] **RACANELLI** (Donata[2] Spano, Vito Antonio[1] Spano) was born in 1933 in Sannicandro, Bari, Italy. She married Domenico Stea in 1958 in Sannicandro, Bari, Italy. He was born in 1928 in Sannicandro, Bari, Italy.

Domenico Stea and Rosalie Racanelli had the following children:

  i. SALVATORE[4] STEA was born in 1959 in Sannicandro, Bari, Italy.

  ii. WALTER STEA was born in 1961 in Monopoli, Italy.

33. iii. MARIA STEA was born in 1965 in Monopoli, Italy. She married Maurizio Clarizio in 1994 in Monopoli, Italy. He was born in Italy.

11. **ROCCO**³ **RACANELLI** (Donata² Spano, Vito Antonio¹ Spano) was born in 1935 in Sannicandro, Bari, Italy. He married Lorraine Orera in 1975 in New York. She was born in 1938 in New York.

Rocco Racanelli and Lorraine Orera had the following children:

34.   i.   ROCCO⁴ RACANELLI was born in 1977 in New York. He married Monica Kumar in New York. She was born in 1980 in India.

      iii.   MICHAEL RACANELLI was born in 1979 in New York.

12. **MARIA**³ **RACANELLI** (Donata² Spano, Vito Antonio¹ Spano) was born in 1940 in Sannicandro, Bari, Italy. She married Gino Stea in 1964 in New York. He was born in 1937 in Sannicandro, Bari, Italy.

Gino Stea and Maria Racanelli had the following children:

35.   i.   ANGELA⁴ STEA was born in 1967 in New York. She married Michael Clifford in 1997 in New York. He was born in 1966.

36.   ii.   PETER STEA was born in 1971 in New York. He married Christen Giuliani in 2000 in New York. She was born in 1974 in New York.

37.   iii.   LISA STEA was born in 1978 in New York. She married Anthony Russo in 1999. He was born in 1977.

13. **ANGELA**³ **RACANELLI** (Donata² Spano, Vito Antonio¹ Spano) was born in 1944 in Sannicandro, Bari, Italy. She married Vito Mossa in 1967 in New York. He was born in 1939 in Sannicandro, Bari, Italy.

Vito Mossa and Angela Racanelli had the following children:

38.   i.   VITO⁴ MOSSA was born in 1967 in New York. He married JENNIFER WOOD. She was born in 1974. He married GERALDINE DERIGGI. She was born in 1971.

39.   ii.   MARIANNE MOSSA was born in 1973 in New York. She married SCOTT CARTER. He was born in 1972.

      iv.   DAVID MOSSA was born in 1978 in New York.

Generation 3 (con't)

40.   iv.   MARK MOSSA was born in 1982 in New York. He married Lindsay Turkov in 2008 in New York. She was born in 1983.

14. **MARIA**[3] **TASSIELLI** (Angela Rosa[2] Spano, Vito Antonio[1] Spano) was born in 1934 in Sannicandro, Bari, Italy. She married Vito Stangarone in 1958 in New York. He was born in 1935 in Sannicandro, Bari, Italy.

Vito Stangarone and Maria Tassielli had the following children:

41.   i.   UMBERTO[4] STANGARONE was born in 1958 in New York. He married Jean Scaglione in 1989 in New Jersey. She was born in 1962.

        ii.   CONSTANCE STANGARONE was born in 1959 in New York.

        iii.   MAXIMILLIAN STANGARONE was born in 1961 in New York.

        iv.   ANGELA STANGARONE was born in 1963 in New York.

42.   v.   SUSANNE STANGARONE was born in 1963 in New York. She married Robert Galvin in 2000 in New York. He was born in 1958 in New York.

43.   vi.   MARTIN STANGARONE was born in 1968 in New York. He married Jodi Rheingold in 1997 in New York. She was born in 1968.

15. **FRANCESCO**[3] **TASSIELLI** (Angela Rosa[2] Spano, Vito Antonio[1] Spano) was born in 1940 in Sannicandro, Bari, Italy. He married Diane Tullo in 1970 in Queens, NY. She was born in 1947 in Queens, NY.

Francesco Tassielli and Diane Tullo had the following children:

FRANK[4] TASSIELLI was born in 1972 in Smithtown, NY.

44.   ii.   SHARON TASSIELLI was born in 1975 in Smithtown, NY. She married Joseph Annese in 2001 in Miller Place, NY. He was born in 1975 in New York.

16. **GRAZIA**[3] **TASSIELLI** (Angela Rosa[2] Spano, Vito Antonio[1] Spano) was born in 1947 in New York, NY. She married Harry Jackson in 1967 in New York. He was born in 1947.

Harry Jackson and Grazia Tassielli had the following children:

      i.   JOSEPH[4] JACKSON was born in 1968.

      ii.   KERRY JACKSON was born in 1969.

45.   iii.   LINDA JACKSON was born in 1971. She married Jeff White in 2001. He was born in 1963.

      iii.   MICHAEL JACKSON was born in 1981.

Generation 4

17. **NICOLA**[4] **MANCHISI** (Gennaro[3], Caterina[2] Spano, Vito Antonio[1] Spano) was born in 1945 in New York. He married (1) **JOYCE GUTTERWELL** in 1966 in New York. He married (2) **LINDA PIZZINO** in 1975 in Michigan. She was born in 1951 in Michigan.

Nicola Manchisi and Joyce Gutterwell were divorced in 1972.
Nicola Manchisi and Joyce Gutterwell had the following child:

      i.   GERARD[5] MANCHISI was born in 1968 in New York.

Nicola Manchisi and Linda Pizzino had the following children:

46.   ii.   NICHOLAS MANCHISI was born in 1976 in New York. He married Shannon Tackett in 2002 in Florida. She was born in 1983.

47.   iii.   ANGELA MANCHISI was born in 1978 in Florida. She married Joseph Glennon in 2005 in Florida.

      iv.   MICHELLE MANCHISI was born in 1980 in Florida.

18. **CATERINA**[4] **MANCHISI** (Gennaro[3], Caterina[2] Spano, Vito Antonio[1] Spano) was born in 1950 in New York. She married Tony Uanino in 1970 in New York. He was born in 1946 in New York.

Generation 4 (con't)

Tony Uanino and Caterina Manchisi had the following children:

48.   i.   ANTHONY[5] UANINO was born in 1971 in New York. He married Shannon Vincent in 1997. She was born in 1972.

49.   ii.   GERARD UANINO was born in 1974 in New York. He married Cindy Harabin in 2000. She was born in 1974.

50.   iii.   CHRISTA UANINO was born in 1977 in New York. She married Corey Quinn in 2001 in Florida. He was born in 1977.

       iv.   MARK UANINO was born in 1980 in Florida. He married Kelly Kelsey in 2012 in Florida. She was born in 1979.

19. **SERENA[4] MANCHISI** (Gennaro[3], Caterina[2] Spano, Vito Antonio[1] Spano) was born in 1953 in New York. She married William MacLellan in 1976 in New York. He was born in 1953.

William MacLellan and Serena Manchisi had the following children:

51.   i.   WILLIAM[5] MACLELLAN was born in 1977. He married Jada Ramsey in 2008. She was born in 1982.

52.   ii.   GERARD MACLELLAN was born in 1978. He married Karen Arnold in 2004. She was born in 1978.

       iii.   JOSEPH MACLELLAN was born in 1981.

20. **MARIA[4] MANCHISI** (Gennaro[3], Caterina[2] Spano, Vito Antonio[1] Spano) was born in 1955 in New York. She married Anthony Coleman in 1978. He was born in 1950.

Anthony Coleman and Maria Manchisi were divorced in 1995.
Anthony Coleman and Maria Manchisi had the following children:

       i.   ROBERT[5] COLEMAN was born in 1984.

53.   ii.   MICHAEL COLEMAN was born in 1987.

21. **CATHERINE**[4] **MANCHISI** (Vito Antonio[3], Caterina[2] Spano, Vito Antonio[1] Spano) was born in 1959 in New York. She married Thomas Englehardt in 1987 in New York. He was born in 1956.

Thomas Englehardt and Catherine Manchisi had the following children:

      i.   THOMAS[5] ENGLEHARDT was born in 1989 in New York.

      ii.   ANTHONY ENGLEHARDT was born in 1992 in New York.

      iii. ANDREW ENGLEHARDT was born in 1998 in New York.

22. **NICOLA**[4] **MANCHISI** (Vito Antonio[3], Caterina[2] Spano, Vito Antonio[1] Spano) was born in 1963 in New York. He married Maria Apostolidis in 2008 in New York. She was born in 1971.

Nicola Manchisi and Maria Apostolidis had the following child:

      i.   ISABELLA[5] MANCHISI was born in 2010 in New York.

23. **MARIANNE**[4] **MANCHISI** (Vito Antonio[3], Caterina[2] Spano, Vito Antonio[1] Spano) was born in 1970 in New York. She married James Smith in 2000 in New York. He was born in 1968.

James Smith and Marianne Manchisi had the following children:

      i.   MARISSA[5] MANCHISI was born in 2002 in New York.

      ii.   LEANNA MANCHISI was born in 2005 in New York.

24. **ANGELA**[4] **MANCHISI** (Vito Antonio[3], Caterina[2] Spano, Vito Antonio[1] Spano) was born in 1978 in New York. She married Salvatore Talluto in 2003 in New York. He was born in 1974.

Salvatore Talluto and Angela Manchisi had the following children:

      iii. ADRIANNA[5] TALLUTO was born in 2006 in New York.

      iv. MATTHEW TALLUTO was born in 2009.

Generation 4 (con't)

25. **LUIGI**[4] **RACANELLI** (Angelantonio[3], Donata[2] Spano, Vito Antonio[1] Spano) was born in 1952 in Sannicandro, Bari, Italy. He married Roseanne Mosto in 1975. She was born in 1954.

Luigi Racanelli and Roseanne Mosto had the following children:
54.   i.   CHRISTINA[5] RACANELLI was born in 1976. She married Christopher Delk in 1998. He was born in 1976.

       i.   ANTHONY RACANELLI was born in 1981.

       ii.   TERESA RACANELLI was born in 1983. She married George Hewes in 2008. He was born in 1981.

26. **VINCENZO**[4] **RACANELLI** (Angelantonio[3], Donata[2] Spano, Vito Antonio[1] Spano) was born in 1953 in Sannicandro, Bari, Italy. He married Anna Barry in 1978 in New York. She was born in 1951 in Ireland. She died in 1996 in New York.

Vincenzo Racanelli and Anna Barry had the following children:
55.   i.   ROSEANNE[5] RACANELLI was born in 1979 in New York. She married Adam Broussard in 2006. He was born in 1979.

       iii.   CHRISTINA RACANELLI was born in 1982 in New York. She married Mario Graziosi in 2011. He was born in 1980.

27. **DINO**[4] **RACANELLI** (Angelantonio[3], Donata[2] Spano, Vito Antonio[1] Spano) was born in 1962 in Sannicandro, Bari, Italy. He married Lillian DiBella in 1996 in New York. She was born in 1969.

Dino Racanelli and Lillian DiBella had the following children:
       i.   SAMANTHA[5] RACANELLI was born in 1999 in New York.

       ii.   ALEXANDER RACANELLI was born in 2002 in New York.

28. **LUIGI**[4] **RACANELLI** (Vito[3], Donata[2] Spano, Vito Antonio[1] Spano) was born in 1954 in New York. He married Nancy Rufrano in 1986 in New York. She was born in 1955.

Luigi Racanelli and Nancy Rufrano had the following children:
     i.   VITO[5] RACANELLI was born in 1988 in New York.

     ii.   JOSEPH RACANELLI was born in 1991 in New York.

29. **JOSEPH**[4] **RACANELLI** (Vito[3], Donata[2] Spano, Vito Antonio[1] Spano) was born in 1961 in New York. He married Kristine Dorritie in 1990 in New York. She was born in 1961 in New York.

Joseph Racanelli and Kristine Dorritie had the following children:
     i.   JOSEPH[5] RACANELLI was born in 1994 in New York.

     ii.   BROOKE RACANELLI was born in 1995 in New York.

30. **ANTHONY**[4] **RACANELLI** (Vito[3], Donata[2] Spano, Vito Antonio[1] Spano) was born in 1967 in New York. He married Amalia Glickman in 1993 in New York. She was born in 1968.

Anthony Racanelli and Amalia Glickman were divorced in 2009.
Anthony Racanelli and Amalia Glickman had the following children:
     i.   AARON[5] RACANELLI was born in 1996 in New York.

     ii.   CARSON RACANELLI was born in 1999 in New York.

     iii. ANGELA RACANELLI was born in 2003 in New York.

31. **JOHN**[4] **RACANELLI** (Vito[3], Donata[2] Spano, Vito Antonio[1] Spano) was born in 1969 in New York. He married Christine Grote in 1999 in New York. She was born in 1969.

John Racanelli and Christine Grote had the following children:
     i.   JOHN[5] RACANELLI was born in 1998 in New York.

Generation 4 (con't)

    ii.   KATIE RACANELLI was born in 2001 in New York.

32. **LUIGI**[4] **RACANELLI** (Francesco[3], Donata[2] Spano, Vito Antonio[1] Spano) was born in 1964 in Sannicandro, Bari, Italy. He married **DANIELA DEPINTO**. She was born in 1965 in Sannicandro, Bari, Italy.

Luigi Racanelli and Daniela DePinto had the following children:
    i.   DONATELLA[5] RACANELLI was born in 1994 in Sannicandro, Bari, Italy.

    ii.   DOMINGA RACANELLI was born in 1998 in Sannicandro, Bari, Italy.

33. **MARIA**[4] **STEA** (Rosalie[3] Racanelli, Donata[2] Spano, Vito Antonio[1] Spano) was born in 1965 in Monopoli, Italy. She married Maurizio Clarizio in 1994 in Monopoli, Italy. He was born in Italy.

Maurizio Clarizio and Maria Stea were divorced in 1998.
Maurizio Clarizio and Maria Stea had the following child:
    i.   CLAUDIO[5] CLARIZIO was born in 1995 in Monopoli, Italy.

34. **ROCCO**[4] **RACANELLI** (Rocco[3], Donata[2] Spano, Vito Antonio[1] Spano) was born in 1977 in New York. He married Monica Kumar in New York. She was born in 1980 in India.

Rocco Racanelli and Monica Kumar had the following children:
    i.   KATE[5] RACANELLI was born in 2008 in New York.

    ii.   JIA RACANELLI was born in 2010 in New York.

35. **ANGELA**[4] **STEA** (Maria[3] Racanelli, Donata[2] Spano, Vito Antonio[1] Spano) was born in 1967 in New York. She married Michael Clifford in 1997 in New York. He was born in 1966.

Michael Clifford and Angela Stea had the following children:

    i.   JEREMIAH[5] CLIFFORD was born in 2000.

    ii.   EMMA CLIFFORD was born in 2001.

    iii.   MORGAN CLIFFORD was born in 2001.

36. **PETER**[4] **STEA** (Maria[3] Racanelli, Donata[2] Spano, Vito Antonio[1] Spano) was born in 1971 in New York. He married Christen Giuliani in 2000 in New York. She was born in 1974 in New York.

Peter Stea and Christen Giuliani had the following children:

    i.   EMILY[5] STEA was born in 2002 in New York.

    ii.   LAUREN STEA was born in 2005 in New York.

    iii.   ISABELLA STEA was born in 2007 in New York.

37. **LISA**[4] **STEA** (Maria[3] Racanelli, Donata[2] Spano, Vito Antonio[1] Spano) was born in 1978 in New York. She married Anthony Russo in 1999. He was born in 1977.

Anthony Russo and Lisa Stea had the following children:

    i.   TAYLOR[5] RUSSO was born in 2002 in New York.

    ii.   PATRICK RUSSO was born in 2003 in New York.

38. **VITO**[4] **MOSSA** (Angela[3] Racanelli, Donata[2] Spano, Vito Antonio[1] Spano) was born in 1967 in New York. He married **JENNIFER WOOD**. She was born in 1974. He married **GERALDINE DERIGGI**. She was born in 1971.

Vito Mossa and Jennifer Wood were divorced in 1999.
Vito Mossa and Geraldine DeRiggi had the following children:

    i.   VITO[5] MOSSA was born in 2005 in New York.

    ii.   NICHOLAS MOSSA was born in 2007 in New York.

Generation 4 (con't)

39. **MARIANNE**[4] **MOSSA** (Angela[3] Racanelli, Donata[2] Spano, Vito Antonio[1] Spano) was born in 1973 in New York. She married **SCOTT CARTER**. He was born in 1972.

    Scott Carter and Marianne Mossa had the following children:
    - i. GABRIELLA[5] CARTER was born in 2003 in Virginia.

    - ii. MIKAYLA CARTER was born in 2005 in Virginia.

    - iii. ISABELLA CARTER was born in 2007 in Virginia.

40. **MARK**[4] **MOSSA** (Angela[3] Racanelli, Donata[2] Spano, Vito Antonio[1] Spano) was born in 1982 in New York. He married Lindsay Turkov in 2008 in New York. She was born in 1983.

    Mark Mossa and Lindsay Turkov had the following children:
    - i. CAMERON[5] MOSSA was born in 2010.

    - ii. AMELIA MOSSA was born in 2011.

41. **UMBERTO**[4] **STANGARONE** (Maria[3] Tassielli, Angela Rosa[2] Spano, Vito Antonio[1] Spano) was born in 1958 in New York. He married Jean Scaglione in 1989 in New Jersey. She was born in 1962.

    Umberto Stangarone and Jean Scaglione had the following children:
    - i. DEAN[5] STANGARONE was born in 1992 in New Jersey.

    - ii. ALEX STANGARONE was born in 1996 in New Jersey.

42. **SUSANNE**[4] **STANGARONE** (Maria[3] Tassielli, Angela Rosa[2] Spano, Vito Antonio[1] Spano) was born in 1963 in New York. She married Robert Galvin in 2000 in New York. He was born in 1958 in New York.

    Robert Galvin and Susanne Stangarone had the following child:
    - i. JACK[5] GALVIN was born in 2000 in New Jersey.

43. **MARTIN**[4] **STANGARONE** (Maria[3] Tassielli, Angela Rosa[2] Spano, Vito Antonio[1] Spano) was born in 1968 in New York. He married Jodi Rheingold in 1997 in New York. She was born in 1968.

Martin Stangarone and Jodi Rheingold had the following children:
-   i.   ABIGAIL[5] STANGARONE was born in 2001 in New York.

-   ii.   CHARLIE STANGARONE was born in 2005 in New York.

44. **SHARON**[4] **TASSIELLI** (Francesco[3], Angela Rosa[2] Spano, Vito Antonio[1] Spano) was born in 1975 in Smithtown, NY. She married Joseph Annese in 2001 in Miller Place, NY. He was born in 1975 in New York.

Joseph Annese and Sharon Tassielli had the following children:
-   i.   ALEXA[5] ANNESE was born in 2002 in Queens, NY.

-   ii.   NICHOLAS ANNESE was born in 2006 in Queens, NY.

-   iii. DANIELLE ANNESE was born in 2007 in Smithtown, NY.

45. **LINDA**[4] **JACKSON** (Grazia[3] Tassielli, Angela Rosa[2] Spano, Vito Antonio[1] Spano) was born in 1971. She married Jeff White in 2001. He was born in 1963.

Jeff White and Linda Jackson had the following children:
-   i.   EMILY[5] WHITE was born in 2003.

-   ii.   ALLYSON WHITE was born in 2004.

Generation 5

46. **NICHOLAS**[5] **MANCHISI** (Nicola[4], Gennaro[3], Caterina[2] Spano, Vito Antonio[1] Spano) was born in 1976 in New York. He married Shannon Tackett in 2002 in Florida. She was born in 1983.

Nicholas Manchisi and Shannon Tackett had the following children:
-   i.   ALEXIS[6] MANCHISI was born in 2002 in Florida.

-   ii.   NICHOLAS MANCHISI was born in 2005 in Florida.

Generation 5 (con't)

47. **ANGELA**[5] **MANCHISI** (Nicola[4], Gennaro[3], Caterina[2] Spano, Vito Antonio[1] Spano) was born in 1978 in Florida. She married Joseph Glennon in 2005 in Florida.

Joseph Glennon and Angela Manchisi had the following child:
      i.   JOSEPH[6] GLENNON was born in 2007 in Florida.

48. **ANTHONY**[5] **UANINO** (Caterina[4] Manchisi, Gennaro[3] Manchisi, Caterina[2] Spano, Vito Antonio[1] Spano) was born in 1971 in New York. He married Shannon Vincent in 1997. She was born in 1972.

Anthony Uanino and Shannon Vincent had the following children:
      i.   KENDRA[6] UANINO was born in 2002 in Florida.

      ii.   MELINDA UANINO was born in 2006 in Florida.

49. **GERARD**[5] **UANINO** (Caterina[4] Manchisi, Gennaro[3] Manchisi, Caterina[2] Spano, Vito Antonio[1] Spano) was born in 1974 in New York. He married Cindy Harabin in 2000. She was born in 1974.

Gerard Uanino and Cindy Harabin had the following children:
      i.   JILLIAN[6] UANINO was born in 2001.

      ii.   GREGORY UANINO was born in 2004.

      iii.   SOPHIE UANINO was born in 2006.

50. **CHRISTA**[5] **UANINO** (Caterina[4] Manchisi, Gennaro[3] Manchisi, Caterina[2] Spano, Vito Antonio[1] Spano) was born in 1977 in New York. She married Corey Quinn in 2001 in Florida. He was born in 1977.

Corey Quinn and Christa Uanino had the following children:
      i.   CARLY[6] QUINN was born in 2005.

      ii.   CAELYN QUINN was born in 2008.

iii. CAMRYN QUINN was born in 2011.

51. **WILLIAM⁵ MACLELLAN** (Serena⁴ Manchisi, Gennaro³ Manchisi, Caterina² Spano, Vito Antonio¹ Spano) was born in 1977. He married Jada Ramsey in 2008. She was born in 1982.

William MacLellan and Jada Ramsey had the following child:
    i. GIANNA⁶ MACLELLAN was born in 2011 in New York.

52. **GERARD⁵ MACLELLAN** (Serena⁴ Manchisi, Gennaro³ Manchisi, Caterina² Spano, Vito Antonio¹ Spano) was born in 1978. He married Karen Arnold in 2004. She was born in 1978.

Gerard MacLellan and Karen Arnold had the following children:
    i. BRADY⁶ MACLELLAN was born in 2006.

    ii. BERKLEY MACLELLAN was born in 2009.

53. **MICHAEL⁵ COLEMAN** (Maria⁴ Manchisi, Gennaro³ Manchisi, Caterina² Spano, Vito Antonio¹ Spano) was born in 1987.

Michael Coleman had the following child:
    i. MICHAEL⁶ COLEMAN was born in 2011.

54. **CHRISTINA⁵ RACANELLI** (Luigi⁴, Angelantonio³, Donata² Spano, Vito Antonio¹ Spano) was born in 1976. She married Christopher Delk in 1998. He was born in 1976.

Christopher Delk and Christina Racanelli had the following child:
    i. MICHAEL⁶ DELK was born in 2011.

55. **ROSEANNE⁵ RACANELLI** (Vincenzo⁴, Angelantonio³, Donata² Spano, Vito Antonio¹ Spano) was born in 1979 in New York. She married Adam Broussard in 2006. He was born in 1979.

Adam Broussard and Roseanne Racanelli had the following child:
    i. LIAM⁶ BROUSSARD was born in 2009.

Epilogue

As I reviewed the contents of this memoir some thoughts came to mind: I doubt I'll ever write another book, and so I want to be as sure as I can be that I haven't made any gross omissions. Was there any significant experience or relationship in my life that I have left out? Was there some memory that remains hidden deep in the recesses of my ancient brain that I'll remember weeks or months from now, and regret it wasn't included in this memoir?

The answer to these questions is, "Probably." Having said that, however, I must let the reader know that there have been many instances when I have stopped whatever I was doing, whether it was reading a book, or watching TV, and closed my eyes, and searched my memory bank, searching for any memory that lies buried in my subconscious. For example, my early childhood years in Sannicandro included significant occurrences (loss of siblings, chronic hunger and sickness), yet none of these experiences have made the transition from my subconscious to my conscious mind. Perhaps that's the way it should be.

Then there are facets of my life that have helped to shape the person I've become: the many jobs I had, beginning with my part-time work in a grocery store when I was twelve years old, my love for and participation in sports, my passion for the New York Yankees, my forty-two year marriage to my beautiful wife, Diane, my son, Frank, whose passion for music I've learned to appreciate, my daughter, Sharon, who brought our three grandchildren into the world and into our lives.

As with any life lived and written about, there are many experiences that will never find these pages, and that is as it should be.

About the Author

As of the date of this publication Frank has been retired for more than eleven years. His life as an educator, as well as the travails and adventures noted in this memoir, are behind him. A new life and a new routine began almost immediately after his retirement in June 2001.

First, he found The Round Table (since renamed OLLI, The Osher Lifelong Learning Institute), a senior educational program at Stony Brook University. Not blessed with hobbies or other diversions to fill his time, Frank learned about this organization and OLLI literally saved his life. The relationships he has formed there are most meaningful to him, and he is deeply enmeshed in its fabric.

Second, he became a grandfather several months after his retirement; a second grandchild arrived a few years later, and a third fifteen months afterwards. Fortunately, their proximity to his home in Nesconset, NY affords him the opportunity to spend a great deal of time with them.

Frank enjoys reading, walking, watching sports on television, especially the New York Yankees, and considers himself somewhat of a movie fanatic.

He may be contacted at cheech40@optonline.net.

17399547R00148

Made in the USA
Charleston, SC ·
09 February 2013